BFI Film Classics

The BFI Film Classics is a serie
and celebrates landmarks of wo... .... Each volume offers an
argument for the film's 'classic' status, together with discussion of its
production and reception history, its place within a genre or national
cinema, an account of its technical and aesthetic importance, and in
many cases, the author's personal response to the film.

For a full list of titles available in the series, please visit our website:
<www.palgrave.com/bfi>

'Magnificently concentrated examples of flowing freeform critical poetry.'
Uncut

'A formidable body of work collectively generating some fascinating insights
into the evolution of cinema.'
Times Higher Education Supplement

'The series is a landmark in film criticism.'
Quarterly Review of Film and Video

'Possibly the most bountiful book series in the history of film criticism.'
Jonathan Rosenbaum, *Film Comment*

The Sound of Music

Caryl Flinn

A BFI book published by Palgrave

To the Baroness

First published in 2015 by
PALGRAVE

on behalf of the

BRITISH FILM INSTITUTE
21 Stephen Street, London W1T 1LN
www.bfi.org.uk

There's more to discover about film and television through the BFI. Our world-renowned archive, cinemas, festivals, films, publications and learning resources are here to inspire you.

Palgrave in the UK is an imprint of Macmillan Publishers Limited, registered in England, company number 785998, of 4 Crinan Street, London N1 9XW. Palgrave Macmillan in the US is a division of St Martin's Press LLC, 175 Fifth Avenue, New York, NY 10010. Palgrave is a global imprint of the above companies and is represented throughout the world. Palgrave® and Macmillan® are registered trademarks in the United States, the United Kingdom, Europe and other countries.

Series cover design: Ashley Western
Series text design: ketchup/SE14
Images from *The Sound of Music* (Robert Wise, 1965), © Twentieth Century-Fox Film Corporation; *The Flying Nun* (Harry Ackerman & Max Wylie, 1967–70), Screen Gems Television; *The Singing Nun* (Henry Koster, 1966), Metro-Goldwyn-Mayer; *Two for the Seesaw* (Robert Wise, 1962), Seesaw Pictures; *Rebecca* (Alfred Hitchcock, 1940), Selznick International Pictures; *West Side Story* (Robert Wise, 1961), © Beta Productions; *How Do You Solve a Problem Like Maria?* (2008), Temple Street Productions; *Mary Poppins* (Robert Stevenson, 1964), © Walt Disney Productions; *Will & Grace* ('Von Trapped' episode, 2006), KoMut Entertaiment/Three Sisters Entertainment/NBC Universal Television; *Moulin Rouge* (Baz Luhrmann, 2001) © Twentieth Century-Fox Film Corporation; *Les Émotifs anonymes* (Jean-Pierre Améris, 2010), © Pan-Européene/StudioCanal/France 3 Cinéma/Rhône-Alpes Cinéma/Climax Films/RTBF; *Mental* (PJ Hogan, 2012), © Mental Holdings Pty Ltd/Screen Australia/Screen Queensland/Screen NSW.

Set by Cambrian Typesetters, Camberley, Surrey
Printed in China

This book is printed on paper suitable for recycling and made from fully managed and sustained forest sources. Logging, pulping and manufacturing processes are expected to conform to the environmental regulations of the country of origin.

British Library Cataloguing-in-Publication Data
A catalogue record for this book is available from the British Library
A catalog record for this book is available from the Library of Congress

ISBN 978–1–84457–474–2

Contents

Acknowledgments

Thanks to the librarians at NYPL Performing Arts Centre, the Library of Congress and the USC Cinematic Arts Library, particularly Ned Comstock. I am very grateful to the Rodgers and Hammerstein Organization for their support and permissions. In particular, Ted Chapin and, especially, Bert Fink have been exceptionally generous in their involvement with this project. My thanks also to the Rackham Graduate School at the University of Michigan for supporting this work with a generous research grant.

Several research assistants aided the writing, including Joseph Deleon, Jessica Getman and Amy Parziale. Above all, however, I thank Joshua Morrison, a PhD student at Michigan, whose research on different aspects of the show, including the songs, helped vitalise the project. His observations regarding the way that orchestration conveyed themes of childhood and maturation will, I hope, be something he pursues in his own work. Kudos to his stellar research and analytical skills, and, it must be added, to his willingness to grow tired of the film.

My gratitude to various audiences who have heard talks based on portions of this book, and to individuals who have in some way helped, including Peter Alilunas, Ralph Bravco, Renee M. Brown, Camille Crichlow-Banning, Steve Cohan, Krin Gabbard, Ann Greenberger, Barbara Hall, Phil Hallman, Kay Kalinak, Kelly Kessler, Al Koenig Jr, Holly Lebed, Adrienne MacLean, Niclas Heckner, Markus Nornes, Katy Peplin, Bart Plantenga, Girish Shambu, Marga Schuhwerk-Hampel, Eric Smoodin, Judy White, Greta Flinn, and Gary and Chester Goertz.

Another round of thanks goes out to individuals who helped during the final months before this book went into production. Among these kind souls are: Richard Abel, Jack Bernard Esq,

Giorgio Bertellini, Eric Brooks Esq, Mary Francis, Desirée Garcia, Bill Germano (who backed this project from the start), Norm Hirschy, Barbara Hodgdon, Dana Polan, Martha Quinn at Fox Corporation, Yeidy Rivero, Matthew Solomon (and 'Auntie Pam'), Johannes von Moltke and Jim Burnstein, without whom this book might never have seen the light of day.

I also want to express my gratitude to other *Sound of Music* aficionados and scholars Julia Hirsch, Raymond Knapp and Richard Dyer for their groundbreaking work on the film. And, from the distance I chose to keep, my appreciation to Julie Andrews and Christopher Plummer for their performances and the pleasure they have given audiences over the years.

1 A Film Classic

As a child, I kept a running list of favourite films that I updated every year, or whenever I saw a new movie that usurped a beloved predecessor. When *Mary Poppins* (1964) came out I went crazy, and my mother contacted Disney Studios. In the mail came a majestic signed black-and-white photo of Julie Andrews, looking wistfully to the edge of the frame. Next year, my dedication skyrocketed when *The Sound of Music* was released. After writing streams of fan letters to Ms Andrews, it dawned on me that the star might not be reading them. Cleverly, I began my next one, 'Dear Julie Andrews. If you are not Julie Andrews, if you are her secretary, please give this to her.' No reply. Reading everything I could on her, I recall how she made her interviewer chuckle with the 'Mary Poppins is a junky' bumper sticker on her car. But I never caught the joke of her return address on the one item I'd received: Julie Andrews, Box 666, Beverly Hills, California.

Christopher Plummer also got my ardent attention. When his Captain von Trapp first sang, I cried, along with legions of others. Indeed, in the massive sea of Plummer, Andrews and *The Sound of Music* fans, I was but one small girl and, then as now, my enthusiasm often pales in comparison to that of others. I'd seen *The Sound of Music* three times (I'd only gone to *Mary Poppins* twice, hence proof), but plenty of people watched it more – a relatively new phenomenon at the time – particularly children and adult women, the film's biggest fan base. One Australian woman, reported Fox, went so frequently that her local theatre decided to let her in for free.

The Sound of Music has a long pedigree: the Trapp story – first recounted by Maria in 1949 – had been made into two German films before Rodgers and Hammerstein's musical opened on Broadway in 1959. Since then, it's enjoyed a revival there, in London and on stages all over the world, including Israel, Russia and Greece – and in countless regional theatres and school productions. In 2013, it was aired on US television in a live broadcast starring country singer and *American Idol* (2002–) winner Carrie Underwood. Trapp publications both real and fictional are available as memoirs, songbooks and even photo albums. Since 1965, Andrews and the seven young 'von Trapps' have turned up repeatedly in interviews and reunions, in DVD commentary, even in state-sponsored events, such as the occasion when the Austrian government decorated the two Trapp families for boosting postwar tourism in Austria. So intermingled have film and reality become that in the 1980s, US President Ronald Reagan played 'Edelweiss' for a visiting Austrian diplomat, believing it was his guest's national anthem.[1]

Its aura remains undiminished. *The Sound of Music* lives on in early twenty-first-century forms like music videos (such as Gwen Stefani's 2006 'Wind It Up'), online, in miniature and manipulated films (historical and imagined auditions, parodies, mash-ups, alternative universe versions, etc.), or in images for a pulpy vampire

A fan's commentary on the 2013 live TV broadcast of *The Sound of Music*; Maria as vampire

novel in which Maria, a hyper-carnal vampire, is a poor fit among Mother Zombie's Abbey. Since 1999, when it premiered at London's Lesbian and Gay Film Festival, *Singalong Sound of Music* has appeared in theatres, encouraging audience participation far beyond 'singing along'. (To illustrate how the film's *economic* aura remains just as undiminished, simply ask any theatre owner who has to rent the *Singalong* print.) Attendees of all ages come in character costume; in addition to dirndl- and lederhosen-clad kids, cross-dressed nuns are common. MCs instruct audiences to hiss at the Baroness and to release their small poppers during Maria and the Captain's first kiss – the inevitable mistimed detonations are best.

There is a lot of financial firepower behind *The Sound of Music*'s position as a film classic. With an original theatrical run of three and a half years, and its figures adjusted for inflation, *The Sound of Music* is still, as of this writing (2015), one of the three top grossing US films – along with *Star Wars* (1977) and *Gone with the Wind* (1939) – with domestic box office at $159 million, excluding sales, rentals, rights and television deals.[2] Just four years after its initial theatrical release, Fox re-released it, and in 1976, when ABC purchased the television rights, they paid an astonishing $15 million for a single showing. For the next twenty years, NBC broadcast *The Sound of Music* twenty-two times, and the film quickly morphed into ritual holiday viewing. The trend wasn't unique to the US, in fact: *The Sound of Music*'s premiere on British TV, just like its premieres in French and German theatres, fell on Christmas Day, becoming a sort of religious relic of its own. In 2000, it was released on DVD and in 2010, in a Blu-ray edition with forty-fifth anniversary extras.

Though a booming business in the 1950s, LP soundtrack sales had fallen off by the next decade as youth-oriented music such as R&B, soul, rock, folk music and protest music became more popular. But none of these new trends affected *The Sound of Music*. Though it was priced higher than other LPs of the period, sales boomed, and the original soundtrack was released in foreign-language versions across

the world. (Fox had taken the unprecedented step of re-recording the songs into different languages when the film was first released abroad.)

The LP's artwork has become a classic, incorporating the same image that was used to publicise the film around the world. The image – not photographic but artistically rendered – melded the iconic picture of Maria on a green hilltop, simultaneously evoking her performances of 'The Sound of Music' and 'Do Re Mi'. Just as she had been when singing 'Music', the joyous Andrews/Maria is prominently and centrally positioned. And, just as in 'Do Re Mi', she is leading her seven young charges, happy in their play clothes, to the top of 'her' mountain. The image seems to lob Renaissance perspective into the dustbin, opting for a near-medieval aesthetics and sense of scale that position Andrews as large and as centrally as it would Christ. The perspective reshapes the children into small, shrunken acolytes and places her poor co-star, the unhappy Plummer, off to the side, where he registers nothing but disapproval.

The giant Maria

Camp and mass appeal

Across their wide demographics, *The Sound of Music* audiences
are known for their repeated, ritualistic viewings and for their
impassioned participation with the film. All the same, it contrasts
sharply to other movies with similar viewers and viewing histories,
such as *The Rocky Horror Picture Show* (1975), whose over-the-top
theatrical indulgences and cynical edges are celebrated by camp
enthusiasts everywhere. *The Sound of Music*, of course, has none of
those features. Nor does it ask for the detachment camp typically
requires, generating its passions through the familiar *closeness* people
have with the film. Coupled with the sincerity of Julie Andrews's
vocal and performance style, and Wise and Lehman's respectful
treatment of the material, *The Sound of Music* is rather resistant to
camp's more detached, sardonic forms – although our Baroness does
begin to flirt with it. The movie is intensely sincere. The acerbic
Richard Rodgers knew that full well, writing to Harold Prince and
Stephen Sondheim on the premiere of their own musical *Company*,
'I think COMPANY is to cynicism what THE SOUND OF MUSIC is
to sentimentality.'[3]

The only way *The Sound of Music* fails to line up as a film
classic is when viewed through the inscrutable lens of High Art:
that it is not, and of course was never meant to be. Coupled with its
supreme sweetness, the film's inability to pass as high culture has
kept academic study of it somewhat at bay. For example, this
volume of the BFI Film Classics appears more than twenty years into
the series, despite the inaugural monograph on *The Wizard of Oz*
(1939), by Salman Rushdie, whose own luminary stature may have
prompted the choice. To be sure, people who dislike *The Sound of
Music* are as numerous as those who love it; many straight men hate
it, intellectuals and guardians of cultural taste hate it, east coast
critics ripped it to shreds, and others refuse any contact with it, as if
it were a bodily contaminant. Christopher Plummer, in fact, spent
much of his long career referring to it as 'The Sound of Mucus' and
trying to keep his distance. It wasn't until 2010, in a special edition

of *The Oprah Winfrey Show* (1986–2011), that Plummer participated in a full cast reunion.

Songs and 'emotional remembrance'

For the fans who enjoy *The Sound of Music*, the trump card is nearly always its songs, whose staying power rivals if not surpasses that of the film itself. From Andrews's unforgettable entrance in the film's opening number, its music reaches out and fixes itself inside of you, whether you know it or not. As Richard Rodgers, whose melodies anchor the film, wrote: 'Once heard, the words, when they are good words, may be superficially forgotten but they are emotionally remembered. The old … competitive cry of the composer, "Nobody whistles the words," is simply not true.'[4] When asked how they decided what parts of a show to put to music and what to leave as dialogue, the pair revealed that they 'used music only when it became impossible to convey an emotional feeling by words alone'.[5]

For audiences, that music of 'emotional remembrance' secures *The Sound of Music*'s status as a classic. Its songs serve the same emotional function in the storyline – comforting scared children, celebrating Liesl's giddy affections, urging Maria to pursue love beyond the Abbey. Of course, the emotional memories evoked by *The Sound of Music* were never the same for the different audiences who have watched it, but it's clear that the film's *target* was to generate a sense of sincere ('authentic') spirit and joy and a G-rated celebration of family and homeland, impressions sustained by Wise's clear-headed direction, European locations that are both credible and lush, as well as Andrews's vocal and acting style.

At the end of the opening credits, the words 'Salzburg, Austria, in the last Golden Days of the Thirties' appear on screen. Despite the precision of the line, the golden letters conscript audiences into a vague but rich emotional sense of time and place, rather than a regionally or historically specific one. Again, this is no small feat for a tale on the cusp of the *Anschluss*. By film's end, as the Trapps trek into

Switzerland – a geographical impossibility – the chorus encourages our joy in knowing that they are following their dream. Not to worry that they're going the wrong way and that they aren't carrying any supplies.

An emotional classic

With this in mind, *The Sound of Music* needs to be considered a 'classic' in a way that hasn't been discussed before: as an *emotional* classic. This 1965 blockbuster tapped a nerve in audiences, whether or not they enjoyed it. Even non-fans were irritated *precisely* because of its unabashed trade in emotion. Pauline Kael infamously called it 'a tribute to freshness that is so mechanically engineered, so shrewdly calculated that the background music rises, the already soft focus blurs and melts, and, upon that instant, you can hear all those noses blowing in the theatre.'[6] As Kael makes clear, *The Sound of Music* has no lofty, heady aims, presuming more simply that feelings – abstracted and universalised, to be sure – seal the contract between film and audience. On that score, *The Sound of Music* aced it. In an interview late in life, director Robert Wise stressed how important it was for film-makers to engross their audiences so that 'they can never escape'.[7]

The musical genre has always exploited the link between music and emotional expression that has dominated western conceptions of music since nineteenth-century Romanticism. While most narrative cinema uses emotion in some manner to engage its spectators, the musical does so in unusually direct ways. Like its close cousin melodrama, the musical strives to involve spectators physically and emotionally in overt appeals that frequently summon the ridicule of viewers, critics and scholars. Like other ostensibly lowbrow genres – horror, porn and melodrama – musicals also prioritise the emotional highs and lows of spectacular sequences over deep narrative and character coherence.

If backstage musicals like *Singin' in the Rain* (1952) depict the excitement of 'putting on a show', *The Sound of Music* went one better by openly celebrating music itself, with songs devoted to the thrill of singing ('The Sound of Music') and of learning to sing ('Do Re Mi'); its most transformative emotional moment occurs when a character who'd *stopped* singing sings again. So, without diminishing the considerable talent behind other aspects of the film, this book maintains that the musical performances anchor most of *The Sound of Music*'s enduring appeal. Thus, after covering some of the film's social, historical, entertainment and industrial contexts – and its fictional and non-fictional precursors – and when we turn to the movie itself, we turn to its songs, to see how they were written and performed, how they function and produce the feelings they do.

Rodgers and Hammerstein

Although secular men, New Yorkers Richard Rodgers (1902–79) and Oscar Hammerstein II (1895–1960) came from Jewish immigrant families. Hammerstein's was steeped in musical theatre. His grandfather, Oscar Hammerstein I, was a risk-taking impresario keen on bringing opera to America. A German immigrant who started off sweeping floors in a New York factory, from the late 1890s to the early 1900s, Hammerstein I worked his way up to building opera and music halls in Harlem and in the emerging Times Square, and helped establish these areas as vibrant theatre districts. Eventually, Hammerstein's entrepreneurial interests shifted from opera to musical theatre, which proved far more lucrative.

Oscar II's Uncle Arthur, a theatrical producer, paired his nephew with established talent and 'gave Oscar the opportunity to hone his skills and make all his mistakes in shows where they hardly mattered'.[8] In 1927, Hammerstein, with composer Jerome Kern, redirected Broadway history with *Show Boat*, a musical that raised issues such as miscegenation and racial passing as it entertained, and did so through vernacular American music and dialogue. *Show Boat* contrasted sharply to the European operetta and revue-derived shows of 'laughter and forgetting' that dominated the Great White Way at the time.[9]

Early in his career, Richard Rodgers wrote songs for musical comedies with the gifted but troubled lyricist Lorenz Hart, generating hits such as 'Isn't It Romantic?', 'Blue Moon' and 'My Funny Valentine'. When he split with Hart, Rodgers approached Hammerstein about collaborating on a show based

Original *Sound of Music* star Mary Martin with (from left to right) Richard Rodgers, Oscar Hammerstein II and writers Howard Lindsay and Russel Crouse (Photo courtesy of Rodgers & Hammerstein: an Imagem Company, 1959)

on the play *Green Grow the Lilacs*, and Hammerstein made musical history a second time. Historians have long stressed the impact that *Oklahoma!*, Rodgers and Hammerstein's first show together, had on Broadway in 1943. It pushed the boundaries of the stage musical by using song-and-dance numbers to work alongside the storyline, rather than to grind it to a halt, and by developing characters rather than using them simply as performance vessels. Though there were obvious predecessors to *Oklahoma!* (not the least of which was *Show Boat*), the show ushered in the era of the 'integrated musical' that prevailed until about the time of *The Sound of Music*, although its dominance has been challenged more often in screen than in stage musical practice.

Rodgers and Hammerstein enjoyed a string of successes, including *Carousel*, *The King and I* and *South Pacific*, and only a few failures (*Allegro*, *Me and Juliet*). *The Sound of Music*, their only show for which Hammerstein did not write the book, would prove their biggest stage hit after *Oklahoma!* It was also their last. During production, Hammerstein was diagnosed with stomach cancer and died, aged sixty-five, on 23 August 1960. Rodgers continued working, though never achieved the same level of success in shows including *No Strings*, *Do I Hear a Waltz?* and *I Remember Mama*. He also proposed ideas for musicals that never took off, such as an adaptation of *The Catcher in the Rye*, and responded to those of others, telling one correspondent in (pre-*Evita*) 1970, 'that the character of Eva Peron could be more exciting and might be a much better basis for a stage piece. Whether or not it's a musical I do not know.'[10]

Of the two, Rodgers was the more irascible personality; Hammerstein was more patient, but with a rigid rationality; both worked hard, to the point of being over-focused and somewhat obsessive. Hammerstein would complain good-naturedly that while it could take him three weeks to come up with song lyrics, Rodgers finished the music in 'an hour or two'.[11] Stephen Sondheim, for whom Hammerstein was a mentor and father figure, described

Hammerstein as a 'man of limited talent but infinite soul'; Rodgers as 'a man of infinite talent and limited soul'.[12] The pair were also savvy businessmen, experts at producing and marketing shows and knowing what details and tricks tended to go over well. They maintained that working on the Broadway version of *The Sound of Music* with Howard Lindsay and Russel Crouse, Mary Martin and her producer husband Richard Halliday went more smoothly than any of their other shows.

Musicals

Even as Fox's adaptation of *The Sound of Music* was going into production, the integrated film musical was losing its dominance. Back in the 1950s, Hollywood had already started to update some of its large musical productions, such as *The Girl Can't Help It* (1956), with cheeky, self-conscious irony, or, in the same film, introducing a rock soundtrack. The industry embraced Broadway's new 'choreographer as auteur' trend, with Bob Fosse and Jerome Robbins finding counterparts in films like Gene Kelly's *American in Paris* (1951). Of course, classical musicals were still being made – such as the adaptations of Rodgers and Hammerstein's shows *The King and I* (1956) and *South Pacific* (1958) – but by the late 1950s and early 60s, the popularity and profitability of musicals began to flatline. Despite efforts to rejuvenate it – notably, *West Side Story* in 1961 – screen musicals were beginning to feel old, especially to young audiences. Icons like Fred Astaire looked more like his partners' grandfathers than their physical equals, and newer musical performers such as Elvis Presley were primarily popular as recording artists, not film stars.

The Sound of Music, Rodgers and Hammerstein's final show, bookended the reign of the 'integrated' musical with which they'd been virtually synonymous. Now integrated musicals were sharing turf with 'concept' musicals, a subgenre that foregrounded unified themes and song types over numbers that fostered narrative momentum. Examples include *Cabaret* (1972), whose songs all

evoked the decadence and unsteadiness of pre-war Berlin, and *Hair* (1979), whose focus on rock counterculture scarcely bothered with storyline at all. *Cabaret* is particularly instructive in this regard, and also shows how musicals' emotional appeals can radically swerve from one show to another. *Cabaret* was roughly *The Sound of Music*'s contemporary and was set in a similar place and time, yet 'Tomorrow Belongs to Me', unlike the equally ardent, anthemic 'Climb Ev'ry Mountain', *intensifies* the creepy, imminent threat of Nazism rather than granting a reprieve from it, hewing more closely to the nascent cynicism and political discontent of much of the West.[13] *Jesus Christ Superstar* (1973) and *All That Jazz* (1979) eschewed family-styled entertainment altogether, courting teen and young adult audiences. Hollywood, while still seeking mass crossover appeal in big-budget productions and roadshows, produced several large-scale musicals with niche audiences in mind, such as *Lady Sings the Blues* (1972), *The Wiz* (1978), *Fiddler on the Roof* (1971) and *Yentl* (1983).

Even more dramatic was the low-budget indie *Easy Rider* that came out four years after *The Sound of Music*. Though not a musical in any pure sense of the word, its soundtrack – with classic tracks by Steppenwolf, Jimi Hendrix and the Byrds – helped establish it as an icon of 1960s counterculture. Subsequent 'New Hollywood' films like *Nashville* (1975), *One from the Heart* (1982) and, later, *Pulp Fiction* (1994) made defining the musical even tougher.

Cover of *The Sound of Music* roadshow booklet, Detroit area (Courtesy of the Donald Hall Collection, University of Michigan. Used with permission)

These same shifts were occurring overseas, most notably in Jacques Demy's *The Umbrellas of Cherbourg* (1964), which re-imagined the very look and sound of musicals. Despite its bittersweet tale of working-class romance, the film's sparkling colours and the near-constant light pop music of Michel Legrand transformed it into what Michel Chion called '*un film en-chanté*'.[14] In the UK, Ken Russell produced extravagantly stylised films in which Liszt becomes a rock star in one (*Lisztomania* [1975]) and Mahler a mordant depressive in another (*Mahler* [1974]). Rock, jazz and other non-Broadway music were anchoring films more and more (*Help!* [1965], *200 Motels* [1971] and *Tommy* [1975]), and the era also saw the rise of 'rockumentaries' such as *Don't Look Back* (1967), *Sympathy for the Devil* (1968) and *Woodstock* (1970).

Beyond its place in the rapidly changing musical, *The Sound of Music* also teetered on the cusp of the 'New American Cinema', released just two years before counterculturally pitched fare such as *Bonnie and Clyde* and *The Graduate*. Within a more global context, the mid-1960s gave rise to innumerable young 'new waves' from Central and Western Europe to Eastern Asia, cinemas intent on rejecting the focus and traditions of their predecessors. These films often tackled social and political problems, using new cinematic languages to do so. In short, they were films willing to take risks. The risk of *The Sound of Music*, on the other hand, was of not taking one. As Bosley Crowther wrote in *The New York Times*, *The Sound of Music* had 'set the musical film back 20 years'.[15]

The revolts, protests and upheavals of the 1960s – the context to which *The Sound of Music* either turned a blind eye or repudiated – took a toll on classical musicals. Critics and scholars have maintained, somewhat tiresomely, that these things even 'killed' the musical, insisting that the genre is by very definition conservative, escapist or overly traditional (their big budgets, for instance, don't always encourage risk-taking in producers) and they fare poorly in tumultuous times.

Since the 1970s, critics have bewailed the demise of the 'classic' musical and its grand icons of the good old days before Broadway became a wasteland pitched to tourists rather than to taste. Authors like Wayne Koestenbaum and D. A. Miller, concerned with gay men's relationship to the musical, share this nostalgia as they expand it, linking gay fandom with the closet, in which musicals, and their cast recordings, could energise the furtive passions of those 'growing up gay' prior to Stonewall in 1969.

Not only does this perspective simplify history (not to mention audiences) by severing present from past but it also idealises the past to contrast it with an ostensibly degraded present. These critics overlook the wide diversity of film musicals produced at the time of *The Sound of Music* (as the alternative musicals listed above show) and neglect the rush of more classic musicals made in its wake. Nineteen sixty-seven alone saw the release of *Camelot*, *Doctor Dolittle*, *The Jungle Book* and *Thoroughly Modern Millie*, three of which referenced *The Sound of Music*'s leading lady: *Camelot* was an adaptation of the stage show for which Andrews received a Tony nomination; *Dolittle* starred Rex Harrison, her co-star in *My Fair Lady*; and Andrews played the lead role in *Millie*. Indeed, the 'death of the musical' view disregards the fact that many of the *current* trends it decries – such as only green-lighting established commercial hits with wide crossover appeal – characterised the same 'good old days' it laments (Mike Todd, anyone?). But naïve or not, this dewy nostalgia typifies a pervasive 'sentimentality' associated with *The Sound of Music*.

That said, *The Sound of Music* is still nothing if not old school. If many consider it to be one of the last great studio musicals, some believe that it was tired from the start. Few blamed the creative team or Julie Andrews – its high production values made sure of that – but instead took aim at its chipper, upbeat tone, its child-centric storyline and naiveté, or simply the fact that it was a musical. According to popular wisdom, by the mid-1960s, traditional musicals were striking a light (and too sweet) note. Even Robert Wise acknowledged, 'if the film had been released two years earlier, or two years later ... we would not have been so successful'.[16]

A decade in turmoil

The Sound of Music was the movie that secured Andrews's lifelong star power and that launched (again, a reluctant) Plummer into mass visibility. But as it assured their futures, for many, the film was bidding farewell to the past in another way, not just as a swan song to the classic Hollywood musical, but to America's comforting postwar illusion that all was right in the world.

    The Sound of Music was an odd duck, emerging at a tangled intersection of film genre, studio history, American political and social life, and amid growing awareness of the Holocaust, Nazism and the US military entanglement in Vietnam. Nineteen sixty-five was thus not simply a challenging moment for Hollywood, but for the country at large, ushering in a period marked by anti-war protests, the Black Panthers, feminists, the summer of love and psychedelia, escalating global corporate structures and economies, debased and alienating working conditions, new demographic and migration patterns, and the decline of white, middle-class, male privilege. Given this context, it is fair to say that part of *The Sound of Music*'s success was in granting conventional, white, middlebrow audiences a swansong of their own with romanticised longings light years away from the world surrounding them. Thus for some, the film's naïve good cheer and resilience have been part of its charm; for others, the basis of its aversion. For an even larger swathe of audiences, *The Sound of Music* simply left them out in the cold, never seeking to address them.

Suppressing the Holocaust

Growing public recognition of the atrocities of World War II provides another historical backdrop to *The Sound of Music*. While cultural and social output in the US lagged behind Europe, the country was far from naïve about the Holocaust. Not only had key books been translated into English – Primo Levi's *If This Is a Man*, Elie Wiesel's *Night* and Anne Frank's *Diary of a Young Girl* among them – but in 1961, the trial of Adolf Eichmann had been broadcast there, as it was worldwide, as a major television event. Thousands of Americans, as Jeffrey Shandler argues, were 'likely to have first heard the word *Holocaust* used to describe the Nazi persecution of European Jewry'.[17]

The Sound of Music eschewed this context. To be sure, so had the Broadway show, but that version *preceded* Eichmann's trial, and in the intervening six years, the public discourse and context had changed considerably. Of course, plenty of other texts were also hiding from the shadow of that past. Over the 1960s, references to the war were appearing across a range of media and cultural forms. Pop culture in particular began trading in recognisable icons of fascism, with Nazi regalia infiltrating subcultural practices like SM erotica and, in more mainstream venues, in movies such as Mel Brooks's *The Producers* (1967), which used the context for laughs. So too did the US sitcom set in a Nazi prison camp *Hogan's Heroes* (1965–71), which took as its backdrop the Holocaust while ignoring its gruesome details. Other mid-1960s series such as *F Troop* (1965–7), *Gomer Pyle, USMC* (1964–9) and *McHale's Navy* (1962–6) poked fun at, if not war, at least military authority. Scholars today are divided over whether such shows were preparing Americans for war, or riffing on the growing *anti*-war sentiment of the time. What is less questioned, however, is how Vietnam provided all of them with an actual historical context and a censored pretext, precisely the same thing that it did, along with the Holocaust and World War II, in *The Sound of Music*.

Today, people tend to simplify and even romanticise the 1960s for its protest movements without considering other competing and contradictory aspects of the decade. One such aspect was a fantasy that, while usually available to children, gave adults a sense of escape, a context filled with fairy-tale romances, hope and pageantry. The year *The Sound of Music* came out, for instance, *Cinderella* (another Rodgers and Hammerstein musical) aired on

US television as a high-profile colour special that introduced the young musical star Lesley Ann Warren to the world. In fact, broadcast network CBS had actually premiered the show (rare for a musical) eight years earlier in an equally big broadcast event – starring a young Julie Andrews.

By the time of *The Sound of Music*, Andrews was completely covered in fairy dust. In addition to her recent turn as a magical governess in *Mary Poppins*, and between the two televised *Cinderellas*, she had starred on stage in Lerner and Lowe's *Camelot* as Guinevere, King Arthur's beloved, adulterous queen. Running for twenty-five months on Broadway, *Camelot* opened the same year that John F. Kennedy, who was a huge fan of the show, was elected President. He and First Lady Jacqueline Bouvier quickly became the country's royal couple and the media seized upon *Camelot* to symbolise the glamour, hope and, in the end, bittersweet story of his short-lived administration. *The Sound of Music* sits squarely in this era. It was first written for the stage before JFK's election, and film

Julie Andrews as Cinderella (1957)

preparations began shortly after his death, when the luminous Kennedy aura had hardly diminished.

This context grounds many of *The Sound of Music*'s fairy-tale aspects: its old European villas, its idyllic imagery of unspoiled nature and, most of all, its cross-class, almost Cinderella-like romance. The 1965 wedding scene between Maria and the Captain is revelatory in this regard, as Andrews – at once Guinevere and Cinderella – walks down the aisle, moving between pageantry and fable, burnishing the film with its strongest fairy-tale component.

Another, lighter, context in which *The Sound of Music* was situated involved the growing visibility of nuns in 1960s popular culture. Although Fox officials had worried that nuns performing popular songs in their film might attract criticism from the Catholic Church (indeed, when broadcast later on French television, those numbers were cut), the risk was attenuated by the fact that so many images of young, spirited and decidedly harmless nuns were cropping up across mass culture. They appeared in films such as *The Singing Nun* (1966) and on TV shows such as *The Flying Nun* (1967–70). Though screen nuns were a relative novelty for the WASPy US, the landscape was changing since the election of the country's first Catholic president (JFK, in 1960), and within the larger global context of Vatican II (1962–5). In an attempt to modernise and widen the appeal of the Church, especially to younger followers, the Second Vatican Council revisited aspects of Church policy – notably by permitting Mass to be performed in contemporary languages.

Julie Andrews as Guinevere in *Camelot* (1960) (AP Photo)

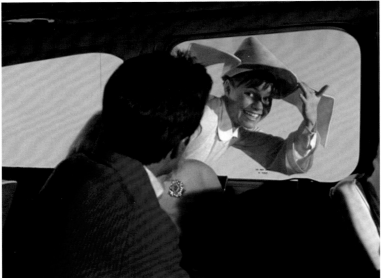

Thus, the 'fun nuns' of *The Sound of Music* and beyond helped burnish Catholicism with the light, vernacular image it sought.

If *The Sound of Music* eschewed the more critical depictions of Catholicism in its European counterparts (for example, *The Devils* [1971]), it nonetheless presents the institutions of Church and State as rather imposing forces. For its story, characters and many of its

Debbie Reynolds as 'The Singing Nun'; Sally Field as 'The Flying Nun' songs are shaped by the Church, and religion is forcefully embodied by Maria, although not in an overtly institutional way; the State is represented by military hero Georg von Trapp. The film is at pains to soften and ennoble these institutions, especially when the characters marry, giving the spunky and simple spirit of the film's songbook a regal but human dignity.

2 Prehistory

The historical Trapps

The story of *The Sound of Music* begins in the nineteenth century.
Born in 1880, Georg von Trapp, the grandson of a naval hero,
became one in his own right when the U-boat he commanded
torpedoed and sank a large, armed French cruiser early in World
War I. The marriage of this national hero to Agatha Whitehead
created a power couple *avant la lettre*, not unlike JFK and Jackie,
or Charles and Diana decades later. Agatha's fortune, like her
husband's, was the bounty of militarism following the invention of
the torpedo by her grandfather, Robert Whitehead. The couple met in
1909 when Agatha christened one of the U-boats Georg would later
command, and once married, their seven children followed in quick
succession, several born while Georg was away at sea.

Maria Augusta 'Gustl' Kutschera described her upbringing as
'that of a wild boy [rather] than of a young lady'.[18] The girl ran
around staircases and slid down banisters, before eventually
becoming a postulate at the Nonnberg Abbey. While there, she was
given a seven-month assignment as governess to young Maria von
Trapp, who had been weakened by the same scarlet fever that had
killed her mother in 1922.

'Gustl' got along well with all the children (she was only
six years older than Georg's oldest son). Unlike her twenty-five
predecessors, she talked with them, darned their socks and, like
their father, sang with them. Of course, *The Sound of Music*'s
Maria has the same energy, drive and ingenuity of her historical
counterpart, but without her leathery toughness. The romance
between Maria and Georg was genuine if not ardent, though it was
assuredly stronger than Georg's decidedly tepid earlier relationship
with a princess.

The Trapp family had always performed music to relax at home. Georg played several instruments and made sure his children did too. He did object, however, when his family started entering competitions, because he didn't want them to sing in public. He was outvoted, however, and they started appearing in wholesome, family-oriented contests and other performances often dressed in traditional dirndls and lederhosen.

Singing would soon prove necessary to the family's finances. Georg had made the mistake of moving his late wife's fortune from a London bank to an Austrian one, and, when the bank failed in 1933, von Trapp – though still the owner of a large mansion – was without funds. Moreover, von Trapp was unable to draw upon his military pension, since he was considered to be a citizen living abroad. (When the Austro-Hungarian empire collapsed after World War I, his birthplace became part of Italian territory.) By the time the military hero left Austria in 1938, the Nazis had frozen von Trapp's assets and seized his Aigen villa, evicting a group of priests whom the Party had displaced once before and to whom Georg had rented his property, symbolically, for a shilling. To add to the family's heartbreak, Himmler used their home as his regional headquarters.

The family fled to Italy, enabled by von Trapp's Italian citizenship, since Austrians were no longer permitted to leave. Interestingly, one of their household staff, an open member of the Nazi Party, had warned the family of the imminent closure of the borders (Wise's film changes this to a betrayal). The family had already been contemplating leaving, so there was no last-minute drama, just a walk to the train station. From Italy, the Trapps went to London, and soon to the US, where they were booked on a singing tour. That engagement proved to be a lifeline when the family – including a pregnant Maria, and Father Franz Wasner, their chaplain, choirmaster and informal manager – were detained by Ellis Island officials, whose suspicions were aroused by their traditional Austrian clothing.

After years of touring, the Trapps settled in Stowe, Vermont, whose rolling green mountains reminded them of home (curiously, they bought the land from a farmer with an ailing wife and seven children). Between tours, they built a compound that evolved organically into an informal inn and, eventually, a ski resort. To this day, the Trapp Family Lodge screens *The Sound of Music* regularly, and family members conduct tours for visitors. Johannes, Maria and Georg's youngest son, maintains the family business, and Georg's great-grandchildren perform as 'The Von Trapps'.

The unlikely coupling of a woman of humble origins with a decorated national hero proved a rich story for the telling. Their ten children (three with Maria), their fame as a singing sensation, and their leaving everything to start a new life spiked the drama even more. Maria's initial account of the family's journey, *The Story of the Trapp Family Singers*, is far more sanguine than those of her stepchildren, who grew to resent the constant touring – they finally outvoted her and dissolved the act in the 1950s. Georg died in 1947 from the same lung cancer that took the lives of his U-boat crew (toxic fumes accumulated whenever their primitive submarine was underwater). Of the family members' many memoirs, Georg's was the only one not centred around domestic life, instead nostalgically recounting his experience as a naval officer and his loss of country.

Die Trapp-Familie

In 1956, German producer Wolfgang Reinhardt, son of stage and screen director Max, bought the rights for Maria's *The Story of the Trapp Family Singers* to adapt into a film. Ruth Leuwerik would star in *Die Trapp-Familie* (1957) directed by Wolfgang Liebeneiner. *Die Trapp-Familie* was an enormous hit, and was followed the next year by *Die Trapp-Familie in Amerika*, a sequel with much of the same cast and crew. For their English-language release, the films were shortened and combined, and, although they performed reasonably well, they did not cause the sensation they had in Germany and Austria.

The German films cover a broader time frame than Wise's later picture and depict more tensions and difficulties, especially as the family struggled in its new homeland. Although not musicals per se, they featured musical performances which resembled the Trapps' actual repertoire far more closely than Broadway show tunes would. Among them was liturgical music, 'Silent Night', children's songs, Austrian *Volkslieder* and a thickly accented rendition of 'Oh Susanna'. Music aside, however, both stage and screen iterations of *The Sound of Music* borrowed liberally from Liebeneiner's movies, replicating scenes such as Maria transforming curtains into play clothes, and others. (Liebeneiner's co-screenwriter Georg Hurdalek receives the curious *Sound of Music* credit for his 'partial use of ideas'.)

Selling Maria's story: the stage musical

When Reinhardt paid Maria von Trapp $10,000 for her story, he made no provisions for her to receive royalties and, she claimed, misinformed her that it was illegal to pay royalties to non-German citizens (it wasn't). She received nothing from the profitable Liebeneiner movies.

Paramount was next to buy the rights, hoping to turn the Trapp story into a film for Audrey Hepburn, but the rights lapsed when the project went unrealised. Vincent Donahue, its future Broadway director, saw the German films and thought they could create a new vehicle for Mary Martin and Richard Halliday. Producer Leland Hayward came on board, obtained the rights and even provided a modest royalty for Maria. Howard Lindsay and Russel Crouse, the venerable writing team, were secured for the book – the story beyond the songs – and Martin herself approached Rodgers and Hammerstein to help with the musical numbers. As Rodgers recalled, the preliminary plan for the music was to use the actual repertoire of the Trapps, and compose only one or two new numbers. He admitted to being mortified, however, by the thought of composing music that would appear alongside titans like Beethoven and Schubert. Ultimately, Rodgers and Hammerstein agreed to write an entirely new score and also signed on as producers, lending another aspect of their expertise to the show.

The Sound of Music premiered on Broadway in November 1959. It was not a critical darling, but it landed several Tonys, including Best Actress and Best Musical, beating no less a figure than Ethel Merman and the more ambitious *Gypsy*. Martin proudly called *The Sound of Music* 'a triumph of audience over critics'.[19] Reviewers generally praised her but were mixed on the score, and frequently grumbled about the show's saccharine, out-of-date character.

Outmoded or not, *The Sound of Music* contained some new, or at least trend-bucking, features. There was no 'eleven o'clock number' to close out the show; even *Gypsy* had included a killer finale in 'Rose's Turn'. Nothing was out of date about its marketing and promotion strategies either: advance box-office sales at the Lunt-Fontanne Theatre topped $20 million (about $40 million in 2015 figures) and the original cast recording sold briskly. Cast members sang or discussed aspects of the show on radio and television before it even premiered, launching it into public awareness. The original run of *The Sound of Music* lasted a rousing three and a half years, closing after 1,443 performances.

A studio in crisis

The Sound of Music was the film that helped save Twentieth Century-Fox. In the 1950s, the studio was full of promise, embracing widescreen early on and releasing apposite, spectacle-driven fare such as *How to Marry a Millionaire* and *The Robe* (both 1953). These and other technologies, such as 3D and stereo sound in theatres, helped Fox stay afloat after the Paramount Decision of 1948, which divested them and other major studios of their theatrical holdings. Making matters worse was the skyrocketing popularity of TV, the rise of suburban audiences and tastes, and the growing cultural and economic clout of youth culture. Fox's winning streak could only go so far, and by 1960 it was haemorrhaging money, with a $2.9 million deficit that year and a $21 million one the next.[20] Then, in 1963, came the Elizabeth

Taylor and Richard Burton epic *Cleopatra*. Although it performed handsomely at the box office and garnered nine Academy Award nominations, *Cleopatra* has gone down in history as an inflated failure. It was a perfect storm of chaos: no final shooting script, ballooning budget (twenty-two times the original by the end), production woes such as emergency surgery for Taylor, last-minute changes in key personnel and the juicy affair of its two married stars. In the end, *Cleopatra*'s box-office grosses failed to recoup its $44 million cost.

By the time *The Sound of Music* went into production, Fox was reeling. In 1962, founder Darryl Zanuck had returned from his overseas retirement partly to depose Spyros Skouras, Fox's President for the past two decades, in the wake of the *Cleopatra* calamity. Zanuck threw his weight behind son Richard, who became the new President, and began laying off over 2,000 employees – staff and contracted stars alike. The pair also shut down production of Fox's iconic Movietone News, and sold off its backlot. By the time *The Sound of Music* was green-lighted, associate producer Saul Chaplin recalled the eerie quiet on the Fox lot, and how no one knew who was in charge of the project.

Still, not everything was a lost cause. Fox's TV shows like *Dobie Gillis* (1959–63) were turning a profit, and Zanuck Sr hit pay dirt with his pet production *The Longest Day* (1962), the gritty D-Day extravaganza that restored reputability to the company and, of course, his leadership.

Prior to *The Sound of Music*, Fox had adapted *South Pacific*, *Carousel* (1956) and *The King and I*, and the studio retained first option for any new shows by Rodgers and Hammerstein. Spyros Skouras went to New York for *The Sound of Music*'s Broadway premiere, attending alongside agent Irving 'Swifty' Lazar (known for his Academy Award parties), who represented Rodgers and Hammerstein and Lindsay and Crouse. Throughout the evening, Lazar watched Skouras like a hawk, 'wanting to gauge the studio chief's reaction to the show. By the middle of the play, Lazar had no doubts. "He was crying like a baby," the agent recalled, "and I knew I had a customer." '[21]

In 1961, Fox secured the rights for $1,250,000. The deal stipulated that the studio couldn't release the film in English-language countries until 'all first class stage presentations of the musical have closed in such countries or December 31, 1964, whichever is earlier'.[22] Unfortunately for Fox, *The Sound of Music*'s extraordinarily long theatrical run left it holding a hot potato precisely when it needed a cash infusion. Smelling blood, Jack Warner approached Zanuck to buy off the rights. Zanuck refused.

Principal production crew

Robert Wise and Ernest Lehman

Director Robert Wise, a studio man, cut his teeth on *Citizen Kane* (1941) as an editor. Known for his even disposition and adaptability, Wise worked in every film genre, though was unhappy with his few Westerns. That range, however, has hampered Wise's status as an 'auteur', and scholars tend to associate the director with workmanlike professionalism rather than with a distinct personality or set of recognisable techniques. 'I've been taken apart sometimes for not having a really conscious style,' he reflected, 'but that's exactly what I wanted. I tried to address each script in the cinematic fashion I think is right for that given script, and since I've done such different kinds of stories, there's no straight stylistic line in my work.'[23]

Despite that variety, Wise, particularly by the 1950s, produced 'a group of crisply realistic, social conscious films' such as *Somebody up There Likes Me* (1956) and *I Want to Live!* (1958).[24] By the 1960s, he gravitated towards spectacle-driven productions such as *West Side Story* and *The Sound of Music*, *The Sand Pebbles* (1966) and *Star!* (1968).

Wise didn't immediately come on board with *The Sound of Music*. When Ernest Lehman, his screenwriting colleague from *West Side Story*, first asked him to join the production, Wise turned him

Robert Wise (centre), with stars Robert Mitchum and Shirley MacLaine from *Two for the Seesaw* (1962) (AP Photo)

down, since he'd begun pre-production on *The Sand Pebbles*.
Lehman then approached Stanley Donen and then Gene Kelly,
who both declined, with Kelly reportedly saying, 'Ernie, go find
somebody else to direct this kind of shit!'[25] William Wyler agreed
to direct but never showed much enthusiasm for it. After scouting
preliminary locations in Austria, Wyler pulled out when Columbia
gave him the opportunity to direct *The Collector* (1954). So Lehman
re-approached Wise, whose *Sand Pebbles* had been delayed,
effectively putting Wise between projects. He agreed. Later, assistant
director Reggie Callow would say, 'It's ironic that he did a favor for
Fox and made himself a multimillionaire.'[26]

    The Sound of Music's staunch and persistent champion,
Ernest Lehman, was one of Hollywood's most accomplished and
successful screenwriters. Over his career, he wrote or co-wrote
dramas such as *The Sweet Smell of Success* (1957), *North by
Northwest* (1959) and *Who's Afraid of Virginia Woolf?* (1966),
and musicals such as *The King and I*, *West Side Story* and *Hello
Dolly!* (1969). Without his enthusiasm for *The Sound of Music*,
it's unlikely the stars would have lined up for the project as they
did, and his expert adaptation of the book transformed the show
about the Trapp family into a more dramatic and far more
cinematic enterprise.

Saul Chaplin

Associate producer Saul ('Solly') Chaplin had got his start in the
1940s at Columbia, working with songwriting partner Sammy Cahn,
choreographer Jack Cole and music director Morris Stoloff on
second-rate musicals. After nine years, he moved to MGM, where he
was vocal arranger for films like *On the Town* (1949) and musical
director for films including *Kiss Me Kate* (1953). For Chaplin, 'the
era of the great MGM musicals' ended 'triumphantly, with Freed and
Minnelli's *Gigi* [1958]. These [Freed] musicals were the culmination
of those made during the 1930s and 1940s.'[27] But Chaplin didn't
abandon the genre, and accepted Wise's invitation to work on *West*

Side Story. (Thus *West Side Story*'s director, associate producer and screenwriter would resume the same roles for *The Sound of Music*. Lehman's colleagues garnered ten Academy Awards for *West Side Story*, but his screenplay failed to win, and for *The Sound of Music*, it was not even nominated.)

The Players
Christopher Plummer

For the role of the Captain, Wise was looking for someone to convey 'Europeanness' and cut a dashing figure. Among the actors considered were Richard Burton, Sean Connery, Louis Jourdan, Yves Montand, David Niven and top contender Bing Crosby, the studio's choice. Thirty-four-year-old Christopher Plummer was largely unproven as a film actor and was known for high-end stage roles such as Cyrano de Bergerac, Henry V and Hamlet. (Julie Andrews was similarly untried on screen, *Mary Poppins* having been shot but not yet released.) Starring in a family musical was hardly a logical career move for Plummer, and he had to be assiduously wooed by Chaplin, Wise and others. Plummer later claimed that he accepted the role for two reasons. First, he envisioned making a musical of *Cyrano de Bergerac* (which he would) and wanted some prior musical experience; and second, he fancied himself 'in a big, splashy Hollywood extravaganza'.[28]

Christopher Plummer as Georg von Trapp

Although Chaplin found the actor to be exceedingly professional, he resented Plummer's attitude. In his memoirs, Chaplin wrote that 'he behaved as though he were a distinguished, legendary actor who had agreed to grace this small, amateur company with his presence'.[29] Still, Plummer's emerging public persona dovetailed beautifully with the film's rendition of von Trapp: urbane, aloof and classy, with a barely submerged sense of eroticism and threat. A big fan of the casting decision was one Maria von Trapp, who expressed her delight over finally having such a handsome husband.

The children

Actors from across the US and, to a lesser extent, the UK, were chosen to play the Trapp children. The only truly recognisable face was English-born Angela Cartwright, who had played Danny Thomas's television daughter in the US show *Make Room for Daddy* from 1957 to 1964. When Angela was hired, Richard Zanuck wanted her to play the girl as a blonde, but lost that argument (as he would many others) to Wise and Chaplin.

American Kym Karath portrayed the youngest Trapp, Gretl. Wise remarked on her 'lovely dark blonde hair' and that she was 'very talkative, a little chubby'.[30] At her audition, the five-year-old stunned Wise and Chaplin by marching right up and announcing, 'I'm here to interview for the part of the youngest child. I'm perfect for it. I can sing and dance and have had lots of acting experience.'[31]

Contenders for Liesl were Kim Darby, Patty Duke, Teri Garr, Lesley Ann Warren and, most famously, Mia Farrow. The team also considered Geraldine Chaplin, but that was nipped in the bud over worries that 'Charlie might be quite difficult'.[32] In the end, Charmian (pronounced Charmy-in, nicknamed 'Charmy') Carr, who had trained as a dancer, was cast, although Chaplin and Wise thought that she looked too old in screen tests. Despite Carr's claims to the contrary, Chaplin states that 'had we known [she was twenty-one], she wouldn't have been considered'.[33]

Rolf

Rolf was one of the last secondary characters to be cast.
Dancer Daniel Truhitte was at a disadvantage with his brown hair.
But when he chose to perform 'Sixteen Going on Seventeen', he
apparently clinched the deal and was signed at a weekly salary of
$400 and quickly subjected to painful, repeated hair dyes.

Max and Elsa
Uncle Max

For Max Detweiler, Lindsay and Crouse recommended pianist-comic
Victor Borge, stating that he 'would add a well-known name and has
great charm'.[34] Wise considered him, along with Cesar Romero and
Hal Holbrook, but knew that hiring the popular Borge would mean
expanding a role he planned to contract. The team finally selected
Richard Haydn, a colourful nasal-voiced comic British actor with
stage, film and television experience, who apparently kept everyone
on set amused behind the scenes.

Elsa Schrader

'Baroness' Eleanor Parker's career began in the 1940s at Warner Bros.,
and she later worked at Fox and MGM (doing a magnificent turn in the
latter's *Home from the Hill* [1960]). Parker was known for two things:
her ability to hide behind an array of characters and performance styles,

Mia Farrow auditions as Liesl

and for being confused with Eleanor Powell. She played a convict in *Caged* (1950), a swashbuckling babe in *Scaramouche* (1952), and sundry other characters, including dancers, spies and cowgirls. Wise was aware that the forty-two-year-old would bring name recognition to *The Sound of Music*. He put it simply to his superiors: 'Eleanor Parker is our most ideal choice in every way for Elsa.'[35]

Her agent fought for better terms than Fox was offering, especially regarding salary, but scored well for her on the credits: 'Miss Parker is to receive billing on a separate card in last position of the entire cast. ... the name of no other player is to be displayed in larger or more prominent type ... with the exceptions of Julie Andrews and/or Christopher Plummer.'[36]

Comic Richard Haydn as Max Detweiler; Eleanor Parker as Elsa Schrader

Oddballs

Max and Elsa are the big misfits in Wise's *The Sound of Music*.
To say that the film diminishes them is an understatement.
On Broadway, the pair had sung two jaunty songs, 'How Can Love
Survive' and 'No Way to Stop It'. But, as Chaplin revealed, 'we
decided that the characters who sang in the stage version should not
sing in the film'.[37]

Of course, in a movie that busily celebrates music, *not* singing
renders Max and Elsa much less important and almost less than
human. With one secondary musical couple thus deposed, the film's
other pairing of Liesl and her messenger boy, Rolf, rises in
importance, screen time and sympathy. In spite of this, 'Uncle Max'
retains significant connections to the film's treasured world of
children and music (as manager, MC, etc.), and even gets a chuckle
or two. But no one, however, is supposed to value the Baroness,
except as an evil, green-eyed monster.

With a vaguely Semitic appearance, and a heavily clichéd
concern about money, Haydn's Max is the only character in *The
Sound of Music* who conveys traces of Jewishness. Curiously, on
stage, the character had carried more ethnic signs, especially as
played by Jewish actor Kurt Kasznar (well-known Jewish singer and
actor Theodore Bikel played von Trapp). Moreover, one of the
numbers Max sang with Georg and Elsa, 'No Way to Stop It', hinted
at klezmer music with its prominent bass clarinet, its bass/chord
rhythms, half steps and dearth of accidentals. That song is but a
ghost in Wise's film, of course, which conveys Max's 'outsider' status
differently, largely by contrasting him unfavourably to von Trapp,
particularly in their responses to Nazism. Unlike Georg, Max will
perform a *Sieg Heil*, even if he childishly wipes his nose afterwards.

Of all the adult leads outside of the Abbey, Max is the only
one without a partner, making him less family or heterosexually
coded than the others. In a revealing, nearly censored moment
filmed at the villa, Georg patronisingly pats Max's cheek after
Max signs up the Trapp children to perform. Zanuck wrote a note

objecting to the gesture, and Wise responded: 'What you feel is "nance" I consider "nuance" in a performance.' (Zanuck also wanted Max and Elsa to get more laughs, to which Wise countered that with Elsa, he needed to show what a disagreeable stepmother she would be.[38])

Elsa Schrader's downfall on film was considerable and deliberate, and its progression can be tracked over her break-up with Georg. On stage, the Baroness ended her engagement after seeing Georg's affections for Maria blossom and, more significantly, after realising his intense anti-Nazism. In Lehman's early drafts, she 'admits defeat by telling von Trapp that she has changed her mind about their marriage ...' and 'gracefully bows out of the picture'.[39] But the final film endows her with no such grace or insight, and audiences take leave of her on the balcony, babbling on materialistically about honeymoons and wedding gifts, clutching to a sinking ship. (Lehman added Elsa's verbal panic late in the game.)

Broadway writers Lindsay and Crouse objected to Wise and Lehman's decision to turn Elsa into Maria's 'rival love interest', complaining that the idea wasn't 'fresh' and made her 'a villainess unnecessarily'.[40] But Wise and Lehman welcomed the drama that a more oppositional figure would give the film.

Lehman curtailed some of the political discussions among Georg, Max and Elsa on stage, despite their utility in explaining von Trapp's break from Elsa. In a scene that was quickly scuttled from his early drafts, Lehman seats Georg, Elsa, Max and Maria together during dinner at Georg and Elsa's party. While engaging in some political banter, Elsa was to have made an unseemly remark, to which 'Maria, who has been too ill at ease to say anything, cannot resist saying something which is highly patriotic' and thus 'scores over Elsa in the Captain's eyes'.[41]

In popular culture, being a failure as a nun is nothing compared to being a failure as a beautiful woman. Consequently, Parker's chilly Baroness embodies an almost-queer, cast-out femininity that is quite alien to *The Sound of Music*'s warm, child-centric world.

The Baroness plays ball

Partnered with the 'nance' Uncle Max, so antithetical is Baroness
Schrader to family life that she can't even throw a ball, and, in
another memorable scene, she seems to be the descendant of one of
Hollywood's most iconic 'deviant' women. As she schemes to unsettle
Maria in her bedroom, Elsa appears to be channelling Mrs Danvers
from *Rebecca* (1940) when the sinister housekeeper intimidates Joan
Fontaine's character while going through Rebecca's intimate apparel
in the dead woman's room.

In contrast to the Baroness, Maria's 'outsider' femininity is
established from the start as so unthreatening that even cloistered
nuns can sing affectionately about it. No such songs celebrate
the Baroness and, in another instance of musical exile, the
underscoring during her final balcony scene with Georg contains
variations of songs that had *never* highlighted Elsa or her
connection to the Captain. Most of the melodies here are taken
from 'My Favorite Things' (pointing to Maria's love for the
children); shorter variations appear from 'Edelweiss' (the Captain)
and 'Something Good' (foreshadowing Georg's duet with Maria).
The only musical concession that the scene makes to Elsa and her
life in Vienna is the waltz metre of the scene's underscoring, but
even that is quickly compromised by the fact that it was the
Ländler (the folk dance performed in waltz time) that anchored the
Captain and Maria's first moment of physical intimacy. As a child,

I scarcely cared about Frau Schrader (though I was mesmerised by her icy beauty); today, I lament the lost Baroness. How thrilling to see her character revived in Laura Benanti's spirited performance in the 2013 version of *The Sound of Music*'s live performance on TV. But a few months later, Eleanor Parker died, at the age of ninety-one.

Judith Anderson as Mrs Danvers in *Rebecca* (1940); Elsa channels Mrs Danvers

Julie Andrews

Robert Wise's extended list of stars to play Maria included Leslie Caron, Grace Kelly and Romy Schneider.[42] Mary Martin was out of the running, having started the stage role at the age of forty-six. But in fact there was no question: it was Julie Andrews all the way. Disney had provided Fox with advance footage from *Mary Poppins*, and Wise and his team were so struck by her screen presence that they knew she was Maria. Fox approached Andrews for the role as part of a five-picture deal, and when her agent baulked, settled on two; the second would be the ill-fated *Star!*, the musical based on Gertrude Lawrence, and also directed by Wise.

Andrews was an ascending star on Broadway, having starred in hit musicals *The Boyfriend*, *My Fair Lady* and *Camelot*. And if less accomplished on screen, she had appeared in the small-screen musical of *Cinderella*. Saul Chaplin always maintained that in Andrews he found a talent comparable to Judy Garland, with whom he had worked on *Summer Stock* (1950) and *I Could Go on Singing* (1963). Both women had grown up in vaudeville and both were solid entertainers who he said possessed a near-magical ability for learning songs instantly. He also found them both to be extremely objective and professional about their work. The differences? Their vocal ranges and singing styles: 'where Judy's voice had great emotion, Julie's has great clarity. When Julie performs, she is always in control and near-perfect every time. With Judy, there was always the worry that she might fall apart at any moment.'[43]

Indeed, Andrews's pure, bright soprano is famous for its crisp enunciation, conjuring a clarity and sincerity that provide the musical equivalent of her star persona. Musicologist Robynn Stilwell describes her voice as 'extremely precise in pitch, timbral clarity, and diction' that reinforce her 'good girl' image while masking the training, work and class privilege behind that impression.[44] (Like Hammerstein's lyrics, 'irony' is not at the heart of Andrews's image, as sex appeal and rebelliousness were not.)

Despite her attractiveness, aspects of Julie Andrews's appearance caused some concern during pre-production. Wise described their first meeting:

We are all crazy about her and I'm sure she is perfect for our show – but she's 5′7″ in her stocking feet so we are going to have to be careful [casting] Elsa, the Captain, and even some of the nuns, so that she doesn't appear too over-sized on the screen.[45]

Casting notes are peppered with annotations about the height of potential co-stars. Today, it's hard to fathom 5′7″ as an aberration, but the film reveals how deeply the concern was taken to heart: throughout the entire movie, Andrews wears only flat shoes. And there were the articles I read as a child about the star's 'huge' feet and size 8 shoe.

3 The Songs of Music[46]

The Sound of Music

The Sound of Music begins in misty abstraction. The wandering camera slowly unveils a series of rugged mountain peaks, stately castles and picturesque Alpine valleys before settling on Maria on the top of 'her mountain'. Screenwriter Ernest Lehman knew exactly what he wanted from the scene. His first screenplay draft begins:

I will tell you the mood, the feeling, the effect that I would like to see. We are floating in utter silence over a scene of spectacular and unearthly beauty … Isolated locales are selected by the camera and photographed with such stylized beauty that the world below, however real, will be seen as a lovely never-never land where stories such as ours can happen, and where people sometimes express their deepest emotions in song.[47]

The film's soundtrack, equally abstract at first, is obscured nearly to the point of silence. It awakens more languorously than the images, with the sound of wind, birds and the stirrings of nature slowly rousing a story and an environment to life. (Films rarely depict worlds awakening via their soundtracks, as *Love Me Tonight* had in 1932.) Lehman's description continues:

faint sounds are beginning to drift up and penetrate our awareness … we are aware that the ground seems to be rising … Our speed seems to be increasing. … Faster and faster we skim the treetops. And then suddenly we 'explode' into: MARIA ON HER MOUNTAIN TOP.[48]

Director Robert Wise packs the 'explosion' Lehman sought with active and kinetic imagery, the aerial shot swooping down to approach Maria, who rushes into the frame, twirling, arms outstretched, face brimming with joy, in one of cinema history's most iconic openings. Yet, on top of this, indeed *before* it even begins, *The Sound of Music* has told us that its soundtrack will be every bit as important.

Lehman had to convince Wise to introduce the film this way. Four years earlier, *West Side Story* (on which the two men had worked together) had also started with a series of helicopter shots establishing its lower Manhattan locale, before gliding up to the projects of the upper west side. Prior to this was a single, abstract, unmoving image. That image, far more abstracted than the fog-filled opening of *The Sound of Music*, contained vertical strokes that seemed to outline the city skyline, behind them, the background colours changing as the overture plays. Once the overture comes to an end, the helicopter moves on to establish a more concrete sense of place, just as it would again in *The Sound of Music*. From its tale of rival urban gangs to Leonard Bernstein's jazz-infused music under its abstract prelude, *West Side Story* immediately conjures a vibrant, youthful present. *The Sound of Music*, by contrast, was more intent on communicating the sense of a grand old world, with images of sublime, unperturbed nature, its 'old school' music, in the traditional Broadway vein, replacing Bernstein's abrupt percussive attacks with the added trills of birds.

Rodgers's music and Hammerstein's lyrics frequently worked to give audiences an emotionally laden sense of place. From *Carousel* to *Oklahoma!* and *South Pacific*, geographically defined communities all informed how each of the stories would unspool, such as when Curly opens *Oklahoma!* singing about the world around him in 'Oh, What a Beautiful Mornin''. Similarly, *The Sound of Music* suffuses its location with a feeling of humble yet joyful awe and a sense of lofty grandeur, not an easy combination to master. The film's success on this front is less the result of any one factor so much as everything falling into place.

The shoot, however, did not. The scouting team had found an approximate location for 'Maria's mountain' in the Obersalzburg

Opening shots of *West Side Story* (1961): abstraction moves to concrete 'place'; opening shots of *The Sound of Music*: abstraction moves to concrete 'place'

region just over the German border in Bavaria. The mountaintop was selected in part for the striking way its long grasses waved in the wind. When the crew returned to film, however, the owner had cut down the field. (Fortunately, the scene was the last one Wise's team shot in Europe, and so the grass had had some time to grow back.) Another challenge was simply getting to the top of the mountain: access proved difficult and the crew had to be brought up by oxcart, along with Andrews, who was photographed riding in one wearing a fur coat.

To move the opening shot quickly onto Maria, the helicopter, with cinematographer Ted McCord, swooped down to the twirling novice, but (as Andrews has repeatedly told interviewers) the backdraught from the chopper blades kept knocking her down, take after take. (No one was assured by the pilot's nickname, 'The Cowboy Pilot'.) Production also involved some last-minute landscaping: the birches Andrews weaves around in medium shot were planted by crew members to give the star something to do as she sang.

In addition to establishing Maria's exuberant personality, this opening number connects her to an unschooled, purely 'natural' joy of singing. In this way, 'The Sound of Music' begins the thematic work of the rest of the movie, anticipating narrative turns down the road, such as the moment music humanises the Captain and, later, when nature offers the family a way out of occupied Austria. 'Music' thus ties Maria to a simple love of country that will later prove compatible with the Captain's own: a nationalism that gives the impression of not being one.

The goals for this opening number are clearly outlined in the instructions Saul Chaplin later wrote for foreign dubbers:

The first words of the song 'the hills are alive ...' should be sung with as much joy and freedom as possible. There should be a gradual diminishing in intensity, so that the middle of the chorus 'My heart wants to beat' is sung as simply as possible.[49]

During the shoot, Andrews, like all of the actors, worked with pre-recorded voices in playback, here and throughout the film, as is typical in most musicals.

The song's uplift and grandeur are established before Andrews ever opens her mouth, when French horns replace the earlier, flightier woodwinds (piccolos, flutes) that had been used to mimic birdsong. Yet Andrews's accompaniment (largely strings and woodwinds) never overwhelms her vocals, nor do the instruments draw much attention to themselves: the focus remains firmly on lyrics and performer. Hammerstein had noted that long, open vowels, when forcefully sung, were effective when paired with high notes, and in that regard 'The Sound of Music' (particularly the word 'music') follows the tradition of his other songs such as 'Bali *ha'i*' in *South Pacific*.[50]

His lyrics also connect nature to religious themes ('larks learning to pray'), celebrating a spiritual presence in nature, as opposed to conventional worship in church. Even the setting helps this, with the number situating Maria's mountain far from the Church, the institution from which she has taken leave that day and whose bells beckon her back. Her more permanent departure occurs later and then, as here, won't involve a full break or rupture from godliness so much as a sanctioned extension of it, with the Mother Abbess urging Maria to extend her love for God through human love on earth.

While some reviewers scoffed at 'The Sound of Music' for what they saw as its corny lyrics, audiences have loved them. Half a century later, in *Singalong* screenings, fans embrace them, bringing words to life in ridiculously literal ways: larks learning to pray are transformed into costumes, as are wild geese flying with the moon on their wings.

The melody of 'The Sound of Music' is deliberately simple. Comprised of almost entirely semi- and whole tones, the song's contour has an undulating feel, evocative of moving water. There are few accidentals, and no dissonant sounds. Its predominantly major chords and harmonies are unembellished, granting the piece a bright

tonal nature and deepening its sense of joyful celebration.
Its repetitive, easily memorised nature augments its straightforwardness,
suffusing the song with a sense of youth and innocence that not all
female vocalists could muster (Ethel Merman, anyone?). In that
regard, Rodgers's music creates an interesting contradiction: its
sense of ease and simplicity allows Andrews's vocal performance to
appear 'ordinary', but at the same time brings its exceptionality into
sharp relief.

Nearly every detail of 'The Sound of Music' showcases its
soloist. A prominent feature is the song's rubato (a slight speeding
and slowing of rhythm used for expressive purposes), which we will
later encounter in 'Climb Ev'ry Mountain'. There, the rubato lends
gravitas, but here, separating the voice from the melodic line creates
a sense of energy and forward momentum that seems to rush
towards the next notes, rather than lingering and giving them weight
as it does in 'Mountain'. Andrews's crystalline voice and crisp
enunciation further brighten and energise the piece with that sense
of anticipation.

Discounting its presence in the underscoring, fragments of
'The Sound of Music' appear twice more: first, when the children
perform it for the Baroness, and their father, overtaken with
emotion, joins in. At this point, the tempo is slower, the chords
blockier, with the 'ahhs' of the children tamping down its initial
brightness. Their thin voices keep any sense of heaviness or initial
grandeur at bay. The second reprise follows Maria's departure,
when the children's voices are weaker still. For this 'sad version',
as production notes refer to it, only the seven children were
recorded. For all of their other songs, Chaplin and arranger Irwin
Kostal added four voices (a few sources say five), including that of
Charmian Carr's younger sister Darleen Farnon, to strengthen the
sound. But because these extra voices were absent in the 'sad'
renditions of 'Music' (and 'My Favorite Things'), the weakened
texture of their singing foregrounds the children's sense of sadness
and loss.

To state that the opening scene of *The Sound of Music* is iconic is to state the obvious. Andrews's Maria presents a striking figure in her novice's costume, arms outstretched, twirling on the top of her hill. The image quickly found its way into public consciousness and became a form of shorthand for *The Sound of Music* itself. It was used in promoting the film and, in a slightly displaced way, also provided the cover of the film's soundtrack LP. Decades later, in both the UK and Canada, *How Do You Solve a Problem Like Maria?* aired as reality TV shows in which contestants competed to star in upcoming theatrical revivals. The CBC promoted their version of the programme with images of a Warholian profusion of twirling Marias, the star's face, and thus her identity, hidden from view.

Opening prayers

At my first *Sound of Music* singalong, when Latin lyrics appeared under the Abbey scenes as the nuns sang liturgical songs, I laughed out loud. It wasn't simply over the top, but it was so deeply at odds with my interactions with the film. My friends and I had *never* sung along to those prayers as children. But here, everyone could, and did.

Following Maria's opening number was no simple task, since odds were so high of a hapless letdown. The solution? Ending 'The Sound of Music' with the chimes of church bells to initiate the film's overture. During this period, overtures typically opened film musicals, but it was less typical to place them *after* the initial number (as Lehman and Wise chose to do), so as not to interfere with the impact of the first scene. Thus, Rodgers's overture plays out as gold-coloured credits roll over a series of scenic shots of Salzburg. To ensure a smooth transition into the hymnal music that follows, Chaplin and Kostal concluded the overture with a brief, recognisable

Multiple Marias promote the CBC reality TV show *How Do You Solve a Problem Like Maria?* (2008) (The image originated with the BBC show that aired in 2006)

melody from 'Climb Ev'ry Mountain', the inspirational number performed by the Mother Abbess.

As was typical for Hollywood, *The Sound of Music*'s production team carefully researched all of the film's references to religion, such as ceremonies, dialogue, and the appearance and comportment of religious figures. The challenge musically was to present the sung prayers as seriously and authentically as possible, for although it was one thing to anger Maria von Trapp, it was entirely another to antagonise the Church. So meticulous were the studio's efforts that Fox sent memos regarding the *kind* of church bells that would chime at the close of 'The Sound of Music' and at the wedding. Then there was the music itself. Rodgers was upfront about his trepidation about composing religious music:

Writing 'Western' songs for *Oklahoma!* or 'Oriental' songs for *The King and I* had never fazed me, but the idea of composing a Catholic prayer made me apprehensive. Given my lack of familiarity with liturgical music, as well as the fact that I was of a different faith, I had to make sure that what I wrote would sound as authentic as possible.[51]

Latin texts were carefully written out for the composer, and a private concert was arranged for him by a local Catholic music instructor in which 'nuns and seminarians performed many different kinds of religious music, from Gregorian chants to a modern work by Gabriel Fauré'.[52]

The result is credible liturgical music. The first hymn, 'Dixit Dominus', is often associated with vespers or evening prayers, and Handel had famously set its text (from Psalm 110) to music in 1707 (small wonder Rodgers was nervous). Following is 'Rex Admirabilis', a matinal hymn from the twelfth century, and then, after more church bells, a rousing 'Alleluia'. Due to its familiarity among lay listeners, 'Alleluia' is indispensable in connoting 'Catholicism' here and across the film; moreover, its air of celebration adorns that Catholicism with a glistening joyfulness.

Maria

Once the nuns conclude the liturgical music, the Mother Abbess engages in a brief exchange with several of them concerning Maria's absence and her questionable future at the Abbey. This exchange softens the transition between a musical number that tries to convey liturgical authenticity and a second that is pure Broadway – 'Maria'. Quite unlike the film's other religious details, 'Maria' doesn't strive for seriousness, something obvious in the conspicuously staged Fox set where it was shot. Musically, in fact, the number has so little to do with religion as to suggest that the ultimate resolution of Maria's 'problem' – her ill fit in the Abbey – will be found outside the Church.

In many ways, 'Maria' anticipates the songs the children will sing. Performing it as if it were a game, the nuns add lines and playfully enumerate Maria's indiscretions, as if trying to top one another. Of course, unlike the children's songs, the youthful playfulness of 'Maria' doesn't characterise its performers so much as its subject, granting Maria not just a quirky vitality, but the affection of her colleagues and, presumably, her audience.

Of course, none of Maria's 'problems' imperilling her prospects for nunhood are catastrophic or create ill will. That lack of threat is highlighted by the orchestration of the song, whose backgrounds are played in light strings and woodwind, with even a perky xylophone after several phrases. The song's background echoes its melody, and the orchestra and voices move back and forth, as if they too were playing a game with each other. Like the film's juvenile numbers such as 'So Long, Farewell' and 'Do Re Mi', some of the phrases in 'Maria' feature arpeggiated chords played staccato.

'Maria' extends some measured gravitas to the Mother Abbess, whose lines are given more strings. Her fuller, more mature singing voice also sets her apart from the five other nuns. One of them, the sweet-faced Sister Margaretta, was played by Anna Lee, a UK-born film and TV actress whose imperfect singing voice Wise found appealing. Evadne Baker portrayed Sister Bernice, and the

stern nun with the long face, Sister Berthe, was played by Portia
Nelson, a singer/songwriter known for her good comic touch.
Other 'nun vocals' included the uncredited, largely off-screen
Beth Lee, the wife of Bill Lee, who would dub for Christopher
Plummer. Curiously, these women who portrayed the nuns were
housed in Salzburg's Bristol Hotel, where they spent evenings with
fellow hotel guest Plummer at the piano, drinking, playing cards
and singing.

The nun of note, however, was Sister Sophia, who sings lines
such as 'But her penitence is real'. Whether intentional or not, the
choice of Marni Nixon to play her was an ingenious way to widen
the showbiz references of *The Sound of Music*. In a very public way,
it also raised the issue of dubbing that scholars have always
considered when studying musicals. Nixon had supplied vocals for
Deborah Kerr in *The King and I*, Natalie Wood in *West Side Story*
and Audrey Hepburn in *My Fair Lady* – the latter being infamously
deemed a 'more bankable' actress whom Warners controversially
cast over Julie Andrews, the star of *My Fair Lady*'s run on
Broadway. Before she was ever hired for *The Sound of Music*, Nixon
was linked to its key players. In addition to Andrews, Nixon was
tied to Rodgers and Hammerstein through her work in *The King
and I* and to Robert Wise through *West Side Story*. That all of her
movie musicals were taken from established stage hits confirmed

Marni Nixon (centre) as Sister Sophia

Nixon as a 'sure bet' for Hollywood's high-stakes, big-budget adaptations during the 1950s and 60s. So by the time *The Sound of Music* came out, audiences now had a face to go with Nixon's voice, something the press gobbled up. Philip K. Scheuer wrote that Nixon was 'now singing as "herself"'; and Hedda Hopper referred to Nixon as 'out in the open'.[53] Fox did nothing to downplay this. In fact, while preparing the film for its distribution abroad, it was Nixon whom they photographed and recorded as a guide for the songs' translators.

Before then, studios rarely informed audiences, even unobtrusively, that roles were dubbed. But even as Fox acknowledged that Nixon did her 'own' singing in *The Sound of Music*, they didn't publicise that Peggy Wood (the Mother Abbess) did not. Bill Lee, who dubbed for Plummer, fared even worse, with Fox contractually requiring him never to receive credit on the film, soundtrack or in any publicity, and to this day many believe they are listening to Plummer's own voice.

I Have Confidence

Rodgers's contract with Fox stipulated that the now-solo composer would write two new songs for $15,000 apiece, whether or not they were used in the final film.[54] The first would replace the Captain and Maria's duet from the play, 'An Ordinary Couple'; the other was simply referred to as the 'Walking Soliloquy'. As Wise recalled, 'Ernie [Lehman] had an idea for what he thought would be a very good place for a new song, when Maria leaves the nunnery and tries to build her courage to face her job at the Captain's home.'[55] Lehman sent some dummy lyrics (below, in part) to Rodgers 'to give some notion of the type, the feel, the emotional level of the song I have in mind':

What lies over the hill I see?
What ... in the world is wrong with me?
Why do I want to turn and flee?
Why am I trembling in the knee?

What is this thing that's come over me?
Why don't I laugh and shout with glee?
Why do I fear to be this free?[56]

The results were underwhelming. When Chaplin visited Rodgers in
New York to hear the two new numbers for Maria, he was impressed
by 'Something Good'; and when Rodgers mentioned the second,
'I Have Confidence', Chaplin recalled, 'A marvelous title ... But then
he played it. What a letdown! It was very short, only sixteen bars,
and in a minor key. There was no joy in it.'[57] The initial lyrics,
moreover, were astonishingly florid.

Once he had returned to Los Angeles, Chaplin carefully
composed a note to Rodgers elaborating his concerns and ideas.
He wanted three parts for the song, beginning with a 'religioso'
opening in the Abbey that Maria '[s]ings dejectedly, "What's the
matter with me?"' The second part accompanies her while
travelling on the bus, its 'music is quasi-recitative' as she 'convinces
herself that everything will turn out fine'; and a third that brings
Maria to the Trapp villa where the music 'is bright and happy'.[58]
Rodgers responded by sending music 'in a fast tempo, in a major
key'.[59] But it satisfied only the third segment of the song, according
to Chaplin, who still wanted content to move Maria from her initial
apprehensive state to her final upbeat one. After consulting
Rodgers, an irritated Chaplin

came to a conclusion: Either he didn't want to write the new material, or he
wanted me to offer to do it. ... After talking on the phone for over an hour,
I capitulated wearily: 'Okay. I'll try writing it. I'll send you a record, and
maybe that'll give you an idea of what I have in mind.'[60]

Chaplin was reluctant for two reasons. First, from a producer's
standpoint, he considered that Rodgers's work was 'incomplete', shy
of what he had promised Fox. Second, Chaplin worried that his own
work, should he compose any, would not match Rodgers's level and

ability. His solution was to take unused music from the show's 'The Sound of Music', which Martin had sung as a first verse, and build lyrics around it. After Chaplin had added lyrics for an extra chorus, Marni Nixon recorded the number, which he sent back to Rodgers for the composer's approval.

The delays with the new songs made Chaplin anxious, especially since Andrews was keen to see her new number. 'I didn't want Julie to know that we were asking her to sing a song that had not been written by Rodgers.'[61] (This is not quite true: correspondence between Chaplin and Rodgers confirms that the two *collaborated* on 'Confidence'.) Still, Chaplin, Wise *et al.* didn't dare inform Andrews of the fact until two years later. She got her gentle revenge, however. Forty years later in the DVD commentary, Andrews states that she didn't understand 'Confidence' lyrics such as 'strength lies in nights of peaceful slumber' and decided to deal with it by performing the number a little 'manic', twirling and spinning as she moved down the road.

The final version of 'I Have Confidence' adheres closely to the three-part pattern Chaplin sought. It starts by playing against a distant background of nuns' voices, laying in a faint 'Rex Admirabilis'. As Andrews moves through the archway (where the real Maria von Trapp appears in a very brief cameo[62]), 'the music changes tempos, hesitates, even becomes amusing'.[63]

Baroness Maria von Trapp's cameo, deep in the background in traditional dress

Appropriately, there is little tonal certainty in this second section, creating a harmonic unsteadiness that matches Maria's own doubts (this portion will appear later in the underscoring when the children test their new governess with frogs).

As Maria's confidence rises, the first stable key of the piece (D major) starts to assert itself, and she moves into the song proper. The keys climb with each quickening modulation, creating energy and momentum that correspond to Maria's own motion. Performed in a rapid 2/4 metre with quick chromatic tones that embellish the melody, the song ends with a dramatic flourish as Andrews sustains her note on 'me' to convey the character's new self-assurance.

Like some of *The Sound of Music*'s other songs, 'I Have Confidence' has a predecessor in earlier Rodgers and Hammerstein musicals. 'Climb Ev'ry Mountain' will conjure up the inspirational 'You'll Never Walk Alone' in *Carousel*, and 'Confidence' recalls 'I Whistle a Happy Tune' from *The King and I*, where another nervous mother-surrogate tries to calm herself as she arrives in an unfamiliar setting to start her new job. 'Confidence' is the more comic of the two, due largely to Andrews's slapstick performance and other comedic moments. Having just convinced herself of her confidence, Maria is overwhelmed by the size of the Trapp villa, and then mistakes the butler, Franz, for the Captain. Literally dwarfed by the scale of the front gate, Maria here recalls Joan Fontaine's infantalised woman as she explores her new home in *Rebecca*. Everything about Rebecca's estate is outsized, the correlate of Rebecca's dominance there, and remains that way for most of the film, whereas Maria's diminishment in *The Sound of Music* is restricted to this early moment.

It was only a year since *Mary Poppins* had been released, and contemporary audiences had fresh memories of Andrews in another quirky get-up carrying an oversize carpet bag like the one she owns in *The Sound of Music*. Lehman's script describes the outfit as 'an ill-fitting unattractive dress and an awkward leather hat'.

'Passers-by', he continues, are 'struck by her odd costume',[64] to which she is oblivious. The Captain is not. After informing him that she relinquished her possessions at the Abbey, including her dresses, she looks down and says, 'Oh – the poor didn't want this one'; and moments later, Brigitta will blurt out: 'I think your dress is the ugliest one I ever saw.' The gag had been part of the Broadway

Dwarfed by the Trapp gate; dwarfed by Rebecca's home

show, which in turn had respected its role in the actual Trapp saga. Eldest daughter Agathe recounts meeting Maria:

we stood in front of a person whose clothes looked as if they had come from a comic book. Gustl ... wore a dark blue summer dress with an unusual neckline, and a leather hat. In one hand she held a briefcase, and in the other hand, a guitar.[65]

Sixteen Going on Seventeen

It is not uncommon to have two couples in a Hollywood musical. In addition to the lead romantic pair, a secondary couple often

'Comic book' dress and carpet bag; with carpet bag in *Mary Poppins* (1964)

provides comic relief or adds 'colour' to the proceedings – think of Edward Everett Horton and his partners in films like *Top Hat* (1935). The couples usually differ in terms of age, class – and hence levels of refinement and perceived 'taste' – ethnicity and nationality. If this secondary couple can widen the demographic appeal of a film, as with Mitzi Gaynor and Donald O'Connor offering youthful counterparts to Ethel Merman and George Sanders in *Call Me Madam* (1953), at the same time they can assuage mainstream anxieties about being different, so that any 'marginal' status they represent seems harmless or well-meaning according to dominant standards and mores. Rodgers and Hammerstein did this with the lower-class fishmonger Mr Snow and his fiancée in *Carousel*, and the young Burmese lovers doomed by their ruler in *The King and I*. Of *The Sound of Music*'s two secondary couples, only the younger pairing, as we have seen, is allowed to sing and be in love.

During the prelude to 'Sixteen Going on Seventeen', Liesl sneaks outdoors to meet Rolf, and when a thunderstorm erupts, they take shelter in a gazebo – not unlike the memorable scene between Astaire and Rogers in *Top Hat*. The number proceeds like a young girl's fantasy. Costumed in a pale, puffy dress, Carr's Liesl looks as if she stepped off the cover of a Harlequin Romance; Rolf is a Ken doll in uniform. Liesl leaps from bench to bench in their balletic dance, and then emits a madcap 'wheeee!' after Rolf kisses her at the end,

'Choreography for horses'

exuding youthful enthusiasm, but not much sophistication on the part of choreographers Marc Breaux and Dee Dee Wood. One film musical scholar calls it 'choreography for horses'.[66]

'Sixteen Going on Seventeen' was the last scene shot in LA after cast and crew had returned from Austria, and Fox recreated the gazebo that had been used in Salzburg. But the artificial rain leaked through the glass panes, and wardrobe neglected to put skids on Carr's shoes. She slipped while shooting, crashing through a glass panel and landing among shards of glass. Despite a badly sprained ankle, Carr finished the scene, her thicker stockings more or less concealing the bandages.

Rolf sings the song's first verse and, once the rain starts and they take shelter, Liesl sings the second. Legato strings play Rolf's opening, with accents by flute, clarinet and woodwind; when Liesl sings, less 'solemn' instruments appear (even xylophone and glockenspiel) to stress her comparative youthfulness. Now the number is less legato, and has more detached, playful notes, and the tension between detached and legato notes can be said to intimate Liesl's own straddling of childhood and adulthood.[67] During the dance segment, the orchestration is extremely active, incorporating large, sweeping flourishes and percussive beats, at once playful and military. But soon the song (always played in a major key) becomes waltz-like, its playful, almost staccato notes diminishing as if to mirror Liesl's own movement from coy flirtation into adult courtship. Towards the end, the volume increases, with musical twirls, accents and crescendi, and the final cadence, played energetically by the full orchestra, seems to mirror the couple's own exhilaration. Rodgers's work, in short, fulfils what Lehman called for in his early scripts when he refers to her dance as 'express[ing] her feeling of independence, her lack of need for a "protector" '.[68]

Much later in the film, having been abandoned by Rolf, Liesl reprieves 'Sixteen Going on Seventeen' briefly with her stepmother. A subtle detail in the song's reappearance shows how assiduously the show sought uncontroversial family fare. Initially, Hammerstein's lyrics closed with references to Liesl's heart and hands being touched; in the end, he chose 'somebody kind who touches your mind', sung by Maria to Liesl. The long 'I's in the rhyme create a sweeter sound and obviate any suggestion of physical intimacy made by the first lyric. The piece, overall, is far more subdued than the version performed in the gazebo; orchestrated now with more strings, and the glockenspiels of the former, which appear on beat at the end of the number, are barely audible here, another detail to reflect Liesl's newfound maturity.

With the initial song's paired characters and gazebo setting (the only romantic location in the film), 'Sixteen Going on Seventeen' clearly anticipates the coupling of Georg and Maria, with both pairs featuring an 'older and wiser' man agreeing to look after a younger, more naïve woman. But when audiences first hear 'Sixteen' at the gazebo, the number forges a romantic promise only to break it: Rolf's lyric 'I'll take care of you' is turned on its head when he later attempts to betray the Trapps near the end of the film. On Broadway, Rolf did not do this.

My Favorite Things

This scene, which was shot on the Fox lot on the second day of production in late March 1964, was the first one between Julie Andrews and the children. Nicholas Hammond (Friedrich) recalls their nerves: 'our very first time in front of the cameras we had to appear as if we were already a tight group'.[69] Andrews quickly put all of the young actors at ease, helping Carr with her cues (which were hard to hear under the thunder sound effects), making funny faces and teaching the younger kids the still-unknown tongue-twister 'Supercalifragilisticexpialidocious'. Recalls Debbie Turner (Marta), 'I remember hopping in bed with Julie ... Here was this perfect stranger, this beautiful woman, giving me a motherly hug and I loved it.'[70]

Ernest Lehman assigned 'My Favorite Things' a new place in the show. For inveterate filmgoers, it is hard to imagine the song performed earlier (between Maria and the Mother Abbess), as it had been on stage. There the Reverend Mother hears Maria singing it, and, recalling it from her own childhood, asks the young postulant to finish the song and joins in. During the storm, the stage Maria had calmed her frightened charges with 'The Lonely Goatherd', a novelty number that Lehman wisely decided to move to a later, less critical moment in the show.

At this point, the Trapp children don't know how to sing, and so Lehman also moved 'Do Re Mi' to a later point in the story so as to respect the plot's logic and enhance its emotional impact. (On stage, Maria had performed 'Do Re Mi' to break the ice when she meets the children for the first time.) Lehman knew it was entirely reasonable for the Trapp children to participate in 'My Favorite Things' as non-singers, calling out lines such as 'pussy willows!'. Pragmatically, using speech eased the transition between talking and singing at the beginning of the number: 'breaking into song' seems less abrupt here. Lehman wanted more of these lead-ins into the songs, believing it to be especially important in 'Favorite Things' with children who don't know how to sing. Andrews also preferred the idea, and Lehman scripted dialogue in which Brigitta and Maria reprise the pre-song banter of Astaire and Rogers once more in 'Isn't This a Lovely Day?', as they muse about the dazzling call and response act between lightning and thunder.

Musically, everything in 'My Favorite Things' works to reassure and calm. Its lyrics, clearly geared to children, are much like the 'list lyric' genre of popular show tunes, epitomised by Cole Porter. Playing in stable 3/4 waltz time, all three beats work as a unit, moving smoothly to the next one, giving the number a subtle 'rush' and forward momentum as it lifts the children's spirits. That lilting pulse is almost physical – waltzes tend to encourage listeners to sway, dance or, here, cuddle and toss pillows. What breaks the beat of 'Favorite Things', appropriately, occurs when lyrics refer to unpleasant things, such as bee stings and dog bites. And the entire proceedings stop cold on the lyrics 'when the dog bites', none too subtly, as the Captain opens the door. Chaplin instructed, 'The last three lines before the Captain enters should be sung as raucously as possible so that the silence caused by the Captain's appearance is a marked contrast.'[71]

Curiously, 'My Favorite Things', a tune about cheering up, is the film's only one performed mainly in minor keys, which to western ears typically feel sad or unsettled. It also includes more modulation than other numbers. Whether or not this makes the piece more challenging to play, or opens up more variations, is a matter of opinion, but it has proved a perennial favourite for performers, especially jazz musicians. In addition to covers by Broadway singers like Barbra Streisand, Dave Brubeck and Sara Vaughn also recorded it.

The cover that looms over all of them, however, is John Coltrane's 1961 version. Capitalising on the minor mode and modulation patterns of 'My Favorite Things', Coltrane went back and forth between minor and major modes throughout the melody, ending not in G major (as the film version does) but in E minor, giving the number more depth and less resolution. Despite assumptions and rumours to the contrary, Coltrane adored the song, telling an interviewer,

'My Favorite Things' is my favorite piece of all those I have recorded ... It's very interesting to discover a terrain that renews itself according to the

'When the dog bites'

impulse that you give it. That's moreover, the reason we don't always play this song in the same tempo.'[72]

Coltrane's peerless renditions have arguably helped make 'Favorite Things' the jazz standard it has become.

Do Re Mi

'Do Re Mi' is a simple song, as indeed it must be, since Maria uses it to teach the children to sing. Its primary scalar patterns make the piece easy to perform, since it lays out the basic form of the major scale through its pattern of half- and whole steps. Despite that formal simplicity, 'Do Re Mi' was the film's most complex number to produce, and the production team allotted more time to it in pre-recording hours than to any other piece.

Preparations were arduous. Andrews and the children, plus the four supplemental vocalists, had pre-recorded 'Do Re Mi', along with 'I Have Confidence', at Fox before shooting began. The recordings were then put on portable tape recorders that Chaplin and Breaux took to Salzburg. There, they worked on staging and timing, going into the streets to time the numbers against traffic lights and calculate how long it would take Andrews and the children to dance down their various paths. This could only be done while the lights were red, which confused local police, who gave up trying to work out what they were doing once they learned that the men were Americans.

Another choreographic challenge was to get Andrews and the children to cycle in formations that mimicked the song's leading voices, patterns and structure. Every movement had to be precise. For the finale on the steps, each step was numbered and every child was assigned a note 'by birth order, descending from the high octave'.[73] Carr recalls, 'We'd shoot five seconds of us patting a statue on the head. Then nine seconds of us running over a bridge. Four seconds marching around the rim of a fountain.'[74]

Despite Lehman's wisdom in resituating 'Do Re Mi' later in the show (he'd scribbled inside Lindsay and Crouse's book, 'She will not win the children over that quickly'[75]), his most virtuosic transformation was in its restaging. By setting the number against a background of outdoor locations, Lehman also extended the performance over time, conveying not merely Maria's growing camaraderie with the children during their father's absence, but giving audiences an attention-grabbing montage number that exploited the Salzburg scenery even more than 'I Have Confidence' had in its own montage.

Hammerstein's lyrics reinforce the instructional nature of 'Do Re Mi' in highly obvious ways; just as Rodgers's music does. In addition to following the form of the major scale, Rodgers's melody stresses the important basic intervals of thirds, fourths and fifths, moving through major triads (do-me-sol-do) that involve a major third (do-mi), minor third (mi-sol) and perfect fourth (sol-do). He even introduces the concept of chromaticism into the song through occasional 'pseudo' modulations in the La and Ti phrases, enabling the young singers to learn the concepts of modulation and chromaticism and adding a small challenge to the song, keeping the teaching tool interesting.

The second half of 'Do Re Mi' introduces the second major melody that is initially sung in solfège syllables ('sol-do-la-fa-mi-do-re ...') into which Maria inserts lyrics, 'When you know the notes to sing ...'. After assigning each child a note of the scale, Maria seems to quiz them during the wagon ride: each sings their note when she

Hitting the high note

points to them with the riding crop. With the conclusion of the
number on the garden steps, each note coincides with the movements
of Andrews and the children, who ascend or descend the steps
according to the rise and fall of the notes. At the top, Andrews raises
her arm overhead and belts out the final note of the song an octave
leap up, an idea she suggested. That final image quickly became
iconic and was featured in roadshow booklets, RCA's original
soundtrack and other memorabilia of the film.

A heavily modified, truncated 'Do Re Mi' is reprised by the
Trapps at the music festival. Unlike its first appearance, when it's
used to teach the children the rudiments of music, the song is now
a showpiece that demonstrates their presentational skills (indeed,
the family's fate partly hangs on their performing it well).
The orchestration is now active, with strong brass and string sounds,
giving the song a denser texture, replete with fanfares and a rare
timpani. There is greater harmonic variety and interest at work, with
the accompaniment straying into minor chords, making the piece
more challenging – and again, more concert-worthy – to sing.
Indeed, the playful, meaningless lyrics in the first iteration of
'Do Re Mi' recede fully into the background at the festival, and even
the family's visual presentation shows their new professionalism and
the serious nature of the song. Clasping their hands in front of their
chests – in the stereotypical manner of operatic solo performances –
the children give unsmiling, emphatic nods to the brass chords of the
orchestra before the final cadence.

Even a small acoustic detail reflects the family's uncertain
predicament in the scene. When the Captain first sings 'jam and bread'
(leading to a new major key), a chord sequence appears before the new
tonic is established, making the modulation here appear less settled.

When the joyful, *initial* rendition of the song was shot and
edited, Wise and his team knew what they had. In fact, 'Do Re Mi'
was the first major sequence they sent back from Austria to the
studio executives and producers, whose telegrams roared with
approval. 'Do Re Mi' played a key role in advance publicity for *The*

Sound of Music, and Fox showed the sequence to backers, press members and potential advertisers on both coasts. And, as Saul Chaplin recalled, even Christopher Plummer 'lost his haughtiness for a few days' after watching it.[76]

The number was equally pivotal in promoting the film after its release, especially for non-theatrical venues for children and their parents or custodians. For instance, publicity man Mike Kaplan suggested using it as a 'short educational film' on TV to teach the basics of music, among other things. 'The film would pay for itself by returning revenue year after year. And every year it would continue to build audiences for *The Sound of Music*.'[77]

The Lonely Goatherd

Even as *The Sound of Music* was being produced for Broadway, 'The Lonely Goatherd' was always called 'the yodel song'. Mary Martin's Maria sang the number somewhat slowly, calming and distracting the children from the thunderstorm; in the film, it is energetically performed for the amusement of the Captain, the Baroness and Max. Shot on the Fox lot after the cast and crew returned from Europe, 'Goatherd' used marionettes on a lavish, portable stage to tell its 'girl meets goatherd' tale.

Zanuck initially wanted 'The Lonely Goatherd' moved into the film's second half, but Wise noted that Maria would have been too distressed by the news of the Captain's marriage to 'join the spirit of the puppet show'.[78] The Salzburg Marionettes, established in 1913 and regionally popular ever since, were first approached to do the number. In the end, Fox hired Bil [sic] and Cora Baird, well known for their puppetry work on television in the 1950s. They had to transcribe Breaux and Wood's 'human' choreography for the puppets (apparently, Breaux and Wood were displeased by the Bairds' adaptation, specifically by the buxom appearance of the female puppets).[79] For three weeks of rehearsals, the Bairds instructed Andrews and the children in the correct movements of a puppet show.

A classic novelty song, 'The Lonely Goatherd' casts two illusions. First, neither Andrews nor the children control the marionettes – the long rehearsal time was largely dedicated to making it *appear* as if they manipulated them. Second, for all of the song's references to yodelling – its thick 'omp pa pa' backbeat, the nonsense syllables of the refrain, the mountains, beer and Tyrolean outfits expressed by lyrics, puppets and stage design – there is no bona fide yodelling in 'the yodelling number'.

Plenty of ink has been spilled about what actually constitutes yodelling, but most agree on two criteria: first is a steep rise or fall between notes – usually in intervals of an octave or a major sixth – that requires the singer to move rapidly from head and chest voices. Second, yodelling entails a discernible, audible 'break' between those voices that is produced through a glottal stop, resulting in the kind of sound one hears in 'uh-oh'. It is this break that distinguishes yodelling from other vocal embellishments. Classically trained singers are taught to *hide* the vocal break and to make transitions between notes as smoothly as possible, no matter the size of the interval, something demonstrated in Judy Garland's famous octave leap in the first two notes of 'Over the Rainbow', in which no break or roughness can be heard.

For some cultural gatekeepers, the vocal 'roughness' of yodelling reflects the supposed 'roughness' or lack of refinement of those who enjoy yodelling. Indeed, in the nineteenth century, as

Tyrolean yodelling became a staple in UK and US music halls, it didn't take long for it to become part of gags and novelty acts. The focus on roughness makes it easy to overlook the real vocal difficulty of yodelling and the training required to do it well. Julie Andrews's friend, comedian Carol Burnett, used a Tarzan-like yodel throughout her career as a calling card, and Andrews herself was undoubtedly capable of performing yodels. But, like *The Sound of Music*, Andrews was not going for robust comedy. So rather than concluding 'The Lonely Goatherd' number with a yodel on the sound-lyrics 'yo de lay he whoo', Andrews performed an interval-skipping embellishment that, while every bit as stylised as yodelling, stems from the other side of the vocal tracks: the operatic tradition of coloratura.

Rodgers toned down the performance demands of 'The Lonely Goatherd' while garnishing it with enough features to make it *feel* like 'a yodelling number'. The nonsense lyrics in the first verse feature only a modest amount of play with the vowels, and 'ay' becomes 'ee', 'o' becomes 'ho', rather than the more typical 'ooo' sound of yodelling. Moreover, the children's enunciation is so smooth and careful throughout that it eschews the fast-paced play of most yodelling.

After Maria and the children finish the puppet show, Maria lets out a big 'phew', an exclamation that Andrews included despite Wise's initial objections. In fact, Andrews inserted bodily punctuation points throughout the film, which, she maintained, made Maria more

Signs of exasperation

plausible and authentic. Other signs of exasperation included sighs, rolling of eyes and running her fingers through her hair – fidgeting gestures that of course stop cold once she becomes Baroness von Trapp. As a child, I wondered why Andrews ran her hands through her hair so much; it struck me as false. It didn't make sense for Mary Poppins to be doing this.

Edelweiss

As his children perform 'The Sound of Music' for Baroness Schrader, the Captain watches from the sidelines and, to their astonishment, joins in and then embraces them. Thus humanised, the Captain is soon cajoled into singing on his own. And so we have 'Edelweiss', his only solo song, and arguably the most moving of *The Sound of Music*'s songbook.

This point may mark the moment in the film that, as Wise claims, his audiences 'can never escape' and in which they are given full permission to care. Although 'Edelweiss' was written as a solo for von Trapp, in his first draft, Lehman had Georg sing portions of 'The Sound of Music' with Maria, as they had in the stage musical, writing that 'when a man and woman sing together, whether they know it or not they are becoming "emotionally involved"'.[80]

Despite the duet not making it to the final cut, 'Edelweiss' clearly establishes the couple's emerging feelings. 'When Georg sings "Edelweiss" here,' reads Lehman's subsequent draft, 'he even falters during the song, so touched is he by Maria's beauty in the flickering light of the fireplace.'[81]

Since the first half of *The Sound of Music* is contingent on von Trapp *not* singing, when he finally does, it is a heartbreaking, tentative affair, the sound of struggling masculinity. And while *The Sound of Music* was not the only musical that tried to 'rewire' or soften masculinity – consider *Mary Poppins* and *Grease* (1978) – it was atypical for positioning that emotionally and narratively laden moment in the middle, and not at the end, of the storyline. Even more curious is that the film's most pivotal emotional moment is given to

the one character who *resists* music – although that resistance is precisely what lends the transformation such affective power. (And von Trapp's resistance to music finds an almost humorous corollary in Plummer's own resistance to 'The Sound of Mucus'.)

Plummer insisted on performing 'Edelweiss' himself, and worked diligently with a vocal coach. Finally, it was determined that his singing was not up to par and Bill Lee, who had dubbed John Kerr as Lt Joe Cable in *South Pacific*, was hired. (It is, however, worth listening to Plummer's respectable recording of 'Edelweiss'.)

During production, Wise noted to colleagues that Plummer agreed with their observation that his character loses strength by singing. Nonetheless, Plummer called his experience of *not* singing 'emasculating'. What he didn't understand was that, like Mr Banks before him in *Mary Poppins*, emasculation was precisely the name of the game, turning an unavailable, authoritarian father into a softer man *present* for his family, a fantasy far removed from the actual experiences of many families of the time. For its version of paternal gentleness and availability, *The Sound of Music* enlisted music every bit as much as it did dialogue and storyline.

In the 1960s as now, the great majority of producers, composers and lyricists of musicals have been men; at the same time, however, conventional masculinity has not been typically associated with music or singing in the way that femininity and women have

Captain von Trapp sings 'Edelweiss' with Liesl

been. Moreover, *The Sound of Music* emerged when a number of Broadway and film musicals featured actors who sang only minimally: *The Music Man*, *Camelot* and *My Fair Lady* all had sing-speaking male leads, largely to accommodate the non-singing stars who played them (Robert Preston, Richard Burton and Rex Harrison, respectively). That trend converged with another of the time: musicals often had *overpowering* female lead characters performed by powerhouse women – for example, *Mame* (Angela Lansbury), *Gypsy* (Merman), *Sweet Charity* (Gwen Verdon) – a feature that critic D. A. Miller maintains widened identificatory opportunities for closeted gay men and boys of the time.[82] For more conventional masculinities, the trend might have been perceived as a form of belittlement. Consider Plummer's critique of the stage characterisation of von Trapp, played by folk singer Thedore Bikel: 'Every time Theodore opened his mouth to say something, Mary Martin would sing 14 verses of a song and drown him out. Here was this man, this great actor, and he had nothing to do.'[83] In fact, Rodgers and Hammerstein composed 'Edelweiss' late, when the show was in tryouts, to provide Bikel with a solo, or 'more to do'.

Not unlike the male speak-singing style of other musicals, Bill Lee's vocal work convinces us precisely for *not* appearing too professional, giving the Captain a sense of subdued authenticity, convincing us that Plummer is doing his own singing. Thus 'Edelweiss', the fake folk song, anchors the sincerity that *The Sound of Music* aims for, and its convincing, contrived authenticity has persuaded many audience members (including President Reagan) to mistake it for a traditional Austrian song.

'Edelweiss' spans a minor seventh, demanding only a modest vocal range. The song's instrumentation is simple: a solo guitar succeeded by soft, unobtrusive orchestration. Its easy, binary structure generates the *feel* of a simple folk song, even though the piece sits squarely in popular song and Broadway traditions. Its intervals are not that typical, nor are they easily sung, and Rodgers provides hints of compositional instability to enhance the song's bittersweet effect. Some of the intervals in phrasing, notably on the lyric 'Edelweiss', give rise to some melodic instability, creating a sense of dissonance in need of resolution. He also positions the tonic note at the edge of the singer's vocal range, not in the more standard – and stabilising – centre, something we hear in the first syllable of 'Blossom'. Taken on their own, none of these details turn 'Edelweiss' into a difficult song or even an unusual one, but collectively, they point to a well-written show tune that requires more vocal talent to perform than the folk song to which it aspires.

Connotatively, 'Edelweiss' is *The Sound of Music*'s only song with traces of political meaning: signalling the 'good nationalism' that Georg embodies, it effectively becomes his leitmotif. Hammerstein's lyrics create a very subtle sense in which that nationalism is informed by notions about gender and ethnicity. For von Trapp, his past and future wives are the figures who bring music into the home, and so their femininity aligns with the domestic aspect of the 'homeland' that 'Edelweiss' strives to 'bless' and preserve. Phrases such as 'blossom of snow' and 'cool and white' provide a glimmer of a national and even ethnic purity, concepts unsettlingly close to the racial purity espoused by Nazism.

'Edelweiss' – a real flower, after all – has nationalist connotations verified by historical fact. As of 1959, the popular Alpine flower appeared on the back of the country's (pre-Euro) Schilling. And earlier, during the war, a little-known resistance group called the 'Edelweiss Pirates' sprang up around German cities. Their members were young, and the names and activities of these organisations often varied by region. These *Edelweisspiraten* committed small acts of insurrection, such as distributing Allied propaganda or producing anti-Nazi graffiti.[84] It is not known whether Hammerstein was aware of this group when he wrote the song.

'Edelweiss' appears for a second time, again at the music festival. Understandably, it loses its intimacy and is more extensively orchestrated. But even as its emotional intimacy is diminished, the song expands 'good feelings' outwards, since Georg's love of country

reverberates in the theatre as the crowd joins in, like an early
Singalong Sound of Music. The group hug that concluded the first
appearance of 'Edelweiss' becomes even larger here, an extended
Austrian family, the audience, conferring its blessing upon a smaller
one about to leave its 'homeland for ever'. To anyone who might miss
the overt emotional and political signage at play here, Wise shows us
the reaction shot from the audience of a deeply irritated Herr Zeller,
the Nazi official in charge of escorting von Trapp to Berlin.

The *Ländler*
The *Ländler* is a traditional Austrian folk dance from the Alpine
region that is performed in waltz time. A festive dance in which

The first *Sound of Music* singalong; the irritated Herr Zeller

couples typically use their hands for twirls and clapping rather than
for close embraces, it is referred to as the 'hand clasping number' in
all of Wise, Chaplin and Lehman's production notes.

At Georg's party for the Baroness, Kurt asks Maria to show him
how to do the *Ländler*. But once his father, who has been watching
from the sidelines, cuts in, the dance assumes the courtship function
we expect when the two leads of a musical dance together. In contrast
to the Viennese waltzes playing indoors at the party, the *Ländler*
takes place in a less formal, exterior setting. Moreover, and just like
'Edelweiss' before it, it intimates a natural and homier expression of
national pride than the waltzes performed in rooms where Nazi
members and sympathisers are among the party guests. But worlds
collide when the ever-vigilant Elsa spies the Captain with Maria and
swoops down.

The *Ländler* is *The Sound of Music*'s only purely instrumental
number. Although diegetically performed at the party (by the Toby
Reiser Quintet, who appear again at the festival accepting second
prize before the Trapps' no-show), this function is nearly
indistinguishable from the piece's presence as underscoring.
Rodgers was renowned for his waltzes, and many consider his
'Carousel Waltz' to be his greatest work. His rendition of the *Ländler*
hews closely to traditional form, maintaining the phrase structure
built on antecedent/consequent phrases of four measures each, and

The 'hand clasping dance'

the major key and down-up-up rhythm. It also shares the close, triadic harmony of traditional *Ländler*, although the film version is performed somewhat more slowly than is typical.

Along with the other waltzes, the *Ländler* had appeared in the Broadway version of the show, but all, especially the *Ländler*, were extended for the party scene in the film. The film's other waltzes here are based on melodies from 'My Favorite Things' and 'Edelweiss', and, curiously, even portions of the excised 'How Can Love Survive'. The latter appears – significantly – when the Baroness returns downstairs after goading Maria to leave. We hear it just as she requests a glass of champagne to 'celebrate'. Only the wedding reprisal of 'how do you solve a problem like Maria?' plays out more humorously.

At first sight, Rodgers's decision to incorporate the melody of 'The Lonely Goatherd' into the *Ländler*'s rhythmic structure seems a curious choice. Why use a novelty children's number at a sophisticated engagement party? Yet it isn't hard to see, for, grand though the scene may be, it lacks the ostentatious dignity of Maria and the Captain's scenes together, whether in the wedding or in 'Something Good'. Crammed with pinched arguments and spiteful behaviour, Elsa's party, in the end, seems a good fit for being underscored with 'Goatherd', the playful but cloying children's song.

'The Lonely Goatherd' also gave the *Ländler* a bounce it would have lacked had it been based on 'Edelweiss', even if the latter might appear to be the more logical choice. Still, 'Edelweiss' is hardly absent in the scene, or elsewhere in the film. In fact, it dominates *The Sound of Music*'s underscoring over and above all other numbers, with the Captain in some way or other cueing its appearance. By contrast, so many songs and fragments reference Maria – no surprise given how many numbers she performs – that the film's overall underscoring has a much less motivic relationship to her than 'Edelweiss' has to the Captain.

Lastly, and like the possible allusion in 'Edelweiss' to *Edelweisspiraten*, the *Ländler* was a savvy choice for its cultural connotations. Historically, members of different classes and social positions – like Maria and the Captain – could perform the *Ländler* together, and the film intensifies this aspect of the dance by placing it alongside other, more elegant waltzes at the ball. Collectively, they function as prized examples of Austrian culture that the Nazis are putting at risk, but within the waltzes, the *Ländler* is shown to be the least politically compromised. For instance, we hear it during the film's few scenes in which von Trapp confronts others, such as his final drift from Elsa, his pointed interactions with Zeller, and even with Max, whom he puts at arm's length for being insufficiently exercised about the Nazis.

So Long, Farewell

Hammerstein readily acknowledged that, unlike fellow lyricists Cole Porter and Larry Hart, comedy and easy wit were not his forte.[85] Still he knew (just as stand-up comics know) that words starting with 'K' can sound humorous to English speakers. As he explained, 'K' sounds, particularly in alliterations, help punch up a song, citing his lyrics 'I'm as corny as Kansas in August' from 'I'm in Love with a Wonderful Guy'.[86] That same 'punched-up sound' also drives 'So Long, Farewell', with its 'clanging' and 'cuckoo clocks', and which treats the lyric 'cuckoo' like a sound effect rather than a word. (A different comic touch occurs when Kurt sings his gender-bending high 'goodbye' at the end of the piece, which was dubbed by Carr's sister Darleen.)

'So Long, Farewell' showcases the children both musically and narratively. Like many of their other numbers, they sing it in front of adults, here at the party; the others they sing *with* adults, notably Maria. But because this moment marks the beginning of their careers as public performers, the children perform 'So Long' on their own.

The orchestration of 'So Long, Farewell' focuses on woodwinds and percussion, with support from strings, and added playful touches of vibraphones and glockenspiels during the children's solos. Due to the song's jaunty, staccato sound, the lines feel light and youthful, without great resonance, full chordal sound or a sense of lingering on melodies or lyrics. More unusual in its orchestration is the prominent use of mallet percussion, although it also appears in numbers dealing with growing up. Here, complemented by a snare drum playing on the offbeats, the mallet percussion adds much to the light, skipping feel of the number, reminiscent of the accompaniment to 'I Have Confidence'.

The song has three sections with distinct tempi, starting with the medium-slow opening passage, an allegro middle and a final section that returns to the slower initial tempo, and continues to slow down until the final goodbye. The central section is quite childlike, with its quick, light tempo and instrumentation, grace notes and other ornamentation, such as an opening xylophone run. But the slower portions, particularly at the end, indicate that this song is really about the children's readiness for bed. By the end, the slowing tempo and increasingly sedate music reflect the sleepiness of its singers.

As with 'Do Re Mi', Rodgers again infuses 'So Long, Farewell' with a playful simplicity, since the children are still relatively new singers. Its melodies are simple, and tend to run up and down the tonic scale of B flat major, emphasising the tonic triad's notes, which repeat throughout. In so doing, the piece subtly references 'Do Re Mi' as if it were applying the lessons Maria had taught them. At the same time, the harmonies underneath the melody are a bit more complex. Non-chord tones remain within the key signature of the tonic key, rather than carrying an accidental to make them fit into the chord outside of the home key, giving the accompaniment an almost modal sound.

Another example of unconventional harmonies occurs with the chords in the xylophone run at the beginning of the song's middle part. These chords are triads with a seventh on top, but without the necessary accidentals to make them 'proper' seventh chords in the key of their tonic. And the final chord of the song (played under the closing 'goodbyes') is written like a tonic triad, with its second tone added and weakening the sense of the dominant. The harmony of this piece differs from the film's other songs, making 'So Long, Farewell' stand out as particularly playful in both content and composition.

The ultimate effect of the contrast between the song's unconventional harmonics and the simplicity of its melody is open to interpretation, but it suggests a tension between the children's rudimentary vocal skills and the more complex, public world they are about to face. 'So Long, Farewell', in fact, is the number that concludes the family's performance at the festival, and also provides the underscoring during the ensuing chase scenes. Musically, the version of 'So Long' that we hear at the festival has not changed much from its performance at the party, although compressed lyrics enable more than one child to leave at a time. While remaining in key areas close to the original B flat major, however, the song features more modulation and harmonic variation here, dipping into minor key areas that underscore the danger the family faces.

Hammerstein's lyrics have the Trapp children 'saying goodbye' first to the partygoers and then to their fellow Austrians. But during the first performance, the song also bids adieu to the *film's* audiences before breaking for the intermission, thereby functioning as the first act 'closing number', minus the usual glitz and fanfare. 'So Long, Farewell' reaches out to audiences in another way too, as it sets the stage for Maria's departure to the Abbey. Attired once more in her ugly dress, she looks back into the room, and at us, before taking her leave.

Maria's farewell

Climb Ev'ry Mountain

Everything about this number works to make a solemn, inspirational impression. Set in a small, enclosed space that Wise favoured for intense emotional scenes, the sequence is enhanced by the dark, chiaroscuro palette of Ted McCord's lighting. Shots are of relatively long duration, with little camera movement, and character movement is similarly kept to a minimum. The Mother Abbess encourages Maria to follow her heart, to 'find your dream', and gives her a literal blessing to pursue romance with the Captain, imparting a spiritual nobility to their relationship.

Rodgers and Hammerstein were no strangers to raising romance to a quasi-religious level: consider their poignant 'You'll Never Walk Alone', performed to the widowed Julie near the end of *Carousel*. 'Climb Ev'ry Mountain', like its predecessor, urges a struggling woman to persevere and move forward, replacing *Carousel*'s 'walking' with 'climbing', which will be directly staged in *The Sound of Music*'s closing shots as the song returns.

On stage, 'Climb Ev'ry Mountain' had been a climactic number, less in terms of scale or staging than for generating a sense of grandeur. It had closed the first act, a crucially important place, since first-act closers – whether large, ensemble numbers or intimate pieces – provide important emotional anchors for audiences and hold them over until the beginning of the second act. In the right hands, 'Mountain' can be a real showstopper, as Audra MacDonald proved in the televised *The Sound of Music Live!* in 2013.

That 'Climb Ev'ry Mountain' exerts such force is curious in light of the fact that Hammerstein believed 'dream' was one of the most overused words in songwriting, along with 'divine'. But as a lyricist, he conceded, 'dream' was simply 'impossible to avoid', because it was too multi-purpose, succinct and easily paired with other words and rhymes.[87]

For the movie, Lehman, Wise and Chaplin wanted to curtail the number's monumentality. They did so by moving it to a later, less prominent place in the story. 'Climb Ev'ry Mountain' would be one of only two new songs to appear in the lengthy, post-intermission part of the film. There were other, pragmatic reasons to diminish the number's grandeur, for throughout pre-production and production, there had been a running question about whether Peggy Wood – who had appeared in musical revues in the 1910s and was more recently known from the TV series *(I Remember) Mama* (1949–57) – would perform her own vocals. In the end, the seventy-two-year-old was dubbed by Margery McKay. Wood liked McKay's voice, finding it similar to her own as a younger woman. But she was no fan of the song and called it 'pretentious'.[88]

As anyone familiar with the film knows, 'Climb Ev'ry Mountain' opens strangely and has few parallels in other musicals. First, there is no dialogue leading up to it. Just as Andrews had requested for 'My Favorite Things', Wood also desired a speaking transition into the number. When Wise asked Rodgers for permission, though, the composer flatly refused, stating that Hammerstein's lyrics were not to undergo any modifications.

And so Wise decided to defuse the pretentiousness that he believed, like Wood, haunted the number. He had Wood start the scene with her back to the camera, and her singing appeared to be directed towards a window near the corner of the room (the choice was not due to Wood's poor lip-synching, as some urban myths maintain). Wise knew the move was controversial, explaining, 'This

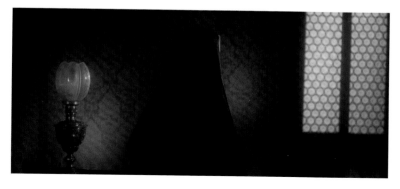

Wise's controversial opening to 'Climb Ev'ry Mountain'

is a very touchy sequence and borders on the corny. I know I was terribly embarrassed by the song every time I saw it on the stage.' But he couldn't cut the number – it was too popular. Instead, 'I've tried to use it more as a "message" for Maria than a number song for our movie audience. There will probably be complaints about our seeming to hide the song, but I feel I'm right in my approach.'[89]

'Climb Ev'ry Mountain' is the only solo sung by a mezzo-soprano, and has the richest sound of the film. (Carr is the other mezzo, but her voice is quite thin in comparison.) In operas and musicals alike, mezzo-sopranos are often cast as mothers, wise women and advisors, a trend Rodgers and Hammerstein had tapped before, with a mezzo performing 'You'll Never Walk Alone' to soprano Julie in *Carousel*. In 'Climb Ev'ry Mountain', the instrumentation strengthens the rich tone colour, depth and resonance of the mezzo. Harps and strings dominate, and the rich bass lines come from cellos and basses, whose full-sounding sostenuto chords make every background chord nearly a show unto itself.

Another feature of 'Climb Ev'ry Mountain' that distinguishes it from the show's other songs is that the soloist's line does not hold to the orchestra. Here, McKay's vocals join the orchestra only in the slow and deliberate finale. The steady, sedate movement, in 4/4 time, creates a rising sense of spiritual uplift over the course of the song that peaks at the end, which is announced by nothing less than trumpets and church bells. McKay's voice ends on a high F sharp, near the top of a mezzo's range, creating an effect quite different from the high notes Andrews, a soprano, hits to close out 'Do Re Mi'.

As the first act's closing number on Broadway, 'Climb Ev'ry Mountain' had garnered plenty of attention from reviewers and was well received. In the film, however, when reviewers identified *The Sound of Music*'s most memorable songs, they rarely included it. Perhaps this was due to the number's less prominent placement in the film, perhaps not. In foreign distribution, for instance, 'Mountain' was the most frequently cut song – audience tests simply found it too slow.

Something Good

Georg is still standing on the balcony when melodies from 'Edelweiss', 'The Sound of Music' and other pieces begin, uniting him and Maria through the underscoring before they even sing a word of 'Something Good' to one another. Prior to this, those numbers had been linked to each character separately, but are now united, sharing a single metre, tempo and orchestration. The most obvious moment occurs when the Captain observes Maria from the balcony; his 'Edelweiss' plays under her image, musically fusing her to him as clearly as his gaze is meant to do.

'Something Good' is the second of the two songs Rodgers wrote without Hammerstein. It is also the second of the show's two love songs, sharing the gazebo and night-time setting with 'Sixteen Going on Seventeen' before it. Yet 'Good' is worlds apart from its predecessor: gone are the thunderstorms, the giddy 'whees' and dance leaps. For 'Good' is a ballad of mature romance. But even as such, it is remarkably unmoving.

The song replaced 'An Ordinary Couple', in which Hammerstein had highlighted Maria and the Captain's desire for sharing a regular routine, emphasising the vernacular worlds and 'regular folk' of so many Rodgers and Hammerstein shows like *Oklahoma!* and *Carousel*. Yet Wise and Chaplin pointed out, not unreasonably, that Maria and Georg were 'far from ordinary' and

Making a link: the Captain gazes at Maria

discarded 'Ordinary Couple' from the film, adding, 'We felt we could get a more romantic piece there.'[90] Rodgers was also not a big defender of 'Ordinary Couple', admitting, 'We wrote that toward the end, when we were finishing up. I think I can do something better than that for you.' Chaplin wanted a 'joyous love song …' Melodically, we asked him to write a long, flowing melody with a very rhythmic accompaniment.'[91]

Played in the key of D flat major, 'Something Good' has no modulations and no major dissonances, a curious decision, since key changes and harmonic dissonances create vital interest and emphasis in a song, and the choice stands in stark contrast with the rapid, upward modulations of 'Sixteen Going on Seventeen'. The orchestration of 'Good' comes almost exclusively from the string section, with few other orchestral colour accents, and no percussion to speak of. That homogeneity separates 'Good' from the other songs, whose orchestration nearly always fosters a sense of playfulness ('Do Re Mi'), local colour ('Edelweiss') or majesty ('Climb Ev'ry Mountain'). Although love songs aren't typically marked by tremendous rhythmic and metrical changes, 'Good' is unusual for containing little rhythmic/ metrical force at all, and for minimising any sense of dramatic arc or movement. It proceeds in a slow, fluid 4/4 time signature, which, despite the liberal use of rubato, does not change. 'Good' is astonishingly calm, and for many, it is the least inspired of the score; musicals scholar Richard Dyer notes its 'lack of conviction'.[92]

Rodgers and Hammerstein had considerable experience writing songs about mature love, notably with their powerful 'Some Enchanted Evening'. The failure of 'Something Good' to ignite may simply be a consequence of appearing in a musical that, unlike *South Pacific*, extols the joys of song and music, not those of adult love. Once coupled, the two leads are beholden to parenting the children rather than enjoying each other's company. That said, *The Sound of Music* was not unique on that front. Numerous TV series and movies from the mid-1960s focused on uniting solo parents for the sake of already-existing children – among them *My Three Sons* (1960–72),

The Parent Trap (1961), *Chitty Chitty Bang Bang* (1968) and *The Brady Bunch* (1969–74) – demonstrating how seriously media industries were taking child-oriented family fare. And, like the fantasy of 'correcting' distant fathers, this pipe dream also gave rise to anxieties about the happy, high-functioning nuclear families that supposedly dominated the era.

Making the extraordinary ordinary

Before losing Georg to Maria, Elsa comments to Max at one point, 'Oh, he's no *ordinary* man,' as if defending the film-makers' choice to ditch 'Ordinary People'. But, of course, musicals frequently deal with extraordinary characters, some even giving them the opportunity to ponder the ways of regular mortals, as Andrews and Richard Burton had done in *Camelot* with 'What Do the Simple Folk Do?' On stage, *The Sound of Music* had actually gone so far as to *showcase* Georg and Elsa's exceptional nature in 'How Can Love Survive', the ironic flip side to 'Ordinary Couple', in which they laugh about the lack of misfortune in their romance. Still, Lindsay and Crouse were careful to check their characters' 'extraordinariness', writing: 'We very early reached a decision … that we had to avoid anything that would make this resemble an operetta, which in America would be disastrous.'[93] And thus they omitted references to Maria and the Captain as Baron and Baroness, and to the Captain's fiancée as a Princess. Their above note was actually written in response to objections raised by Baroness von Trapp, who was aggrieved that her and her husband's titles had been dropped. Lindsay and Crouse were right, of course: the tale's operetta-like aspects had to go, as did its honorific, aristocratic titles. Baroness Schrader is the only lead character to retain hers, and we know where that gets her.

Indeed, American audiences can take only so much appeal to privilege, so downplaying von Trapp's wealth and status was critical for box-office success. The move also helped shore up the film's sense of joyfulness by igniting the popular fiction that true happiness stems from ordinary experiences of regular folk – indeed, the lyrics in

'I Have Confidence' say as much. Of course, to cover their bets, if the show's creative team couldn't stress the aristocratic 'operetta', they *could* foreground the fairy-tale-like rewards reaped by Maria, and so they did. In the end, though, for as difficult as it is to consider Maria and the Captain as an 'ordinary couple', it's even more of a stretch to imagine Maria having had a 'wicked' or 'miserable' past, as Rodgers's lyrics for 'Something Good' might have us believe.

While filming, Plummer and Andrews could not keep from laughing. 'Something Good' was one of the last numbers shot at Fox after the crew had returned from Austria, and exhaustion might have been a factor. But the ageing carbon inside the klieg lights on set was making 'a terrible noise, like a groan or, more often, a raspberry'. 'It was like a comment on our scene!' said Andrews. 'Well, Chris and I would start laughing. We couldn't help it.'[94] After many failed takes, Wise told them to gather their composure over lunch, but when the noises resumed, they lost it all over again. So Wise shot the scene in silhouette. If his actors kept on cackling, he reasoned, at least their smiles wouldn't be detectable.

Wedding processional

Like 'The Sound of Music', Maria and the Captain's wedding scene aims for grand spectacle, generated here through rich pageantry rather than sublime nature. One of the few interiors filmed on

The giggling co-stars

location, at the Mondsee Cathedral, this was the first scene shot in Europe, and was completed in a single day.

Lehman's script instructed, 'There is no dialogue in this scene,' having it unfold as a production number, though without singing and dancing, but still presenting a feast for audiences to consume.[95] There *is* singing, of course, in the form of a huge female choir, and choreography, as the wedding party moves down the aisle, but overall the scene comes across less as a musical number than as something akin to grand historical weddings, whether those of royalty, JFK and Jackie, or, perhaps, Georg and Agatha von Trapp.

Wise used few close-ups, subordinating intimacy to large-scale impressions and feelings of awe, not unlike 'The Sound of Music' in that regard. Long overhead shots capture the procession, and additional cameras shoot from behind church columns, as if they too were among the throngs of well-wishers and witnesses. As Andrews/Maria prepares to walk down the aisle, the organ plays a hymn-like passage and then – famously – has the choir reprise 'Maria'. Since the moment *The Sound of Music* hit the screen, many audience members, including myself, found this bizarre, and it's a testament to Robert Wise's direction that the reverent grandeur of the sequence dispels the laughter that such a risible song reprisal might have induced.

In this scene, *The Sound of Music* combines the institutions of state and religion somewhat literally, by marrying its two

Fairy-tale wedding

representatives. The music follows the very same path, with a slow quasi-military march accompanying Maria as she moves down the aisle of the cathedral. 'The aim', as Chaplin said, 'is to get the contrast between the martial music of the accompaniment and the sweet simple singing of the nuns.'[96]

The five singing 'nuns' had pre-recorded their vocals, but only Anna Lee, Portia Nelson and Peggy Wood took part in the actual filming in Salzburg, reducing Marni Nixon to an unseen voice once more (this irony didn't escape her, as she notes in her autobiography[97]). A further twenty-four female vocalists were added, giving the choir an even thicker, lush sound.

The organ thoroughly dominates the number, just as it had done in 'Climb Ev'ry Mountain', where it also worked to merge religion and romance. The brass section is quite pronounced as well, lending phrases a fanfare quality in addition to laying down the march-like rhythm that curbs and regulates the pace of 'Maria'. The chimes of church bells offer punctuation marks to highlight the spectacle's liturgical significance, and glockenspiel and snare drums (previously used in 'Sixteen Going on Seventeen' to very different effect) foreground the military dimensions of the wedding, the latter sartorially represented by the Captain and his formal uniform. In the end, though, the Church (and hence Maria) trumps the military: in the scene's triumphant finale, Wise's camera tilts to move up from the couple to the top of the church, to its steeple bells, and then celestially into the sky.

No musical honeymoon

Most musicals, fairy-tale ones especially, don't depict the lives of their characters after their weddings. *The Sound of Music* does, however, and comes to a screeching halt in the process. It doesn't become 'serious' after the marriage so much as seriously unfun. For, if Maria brought music back into the Trapp house, once *she* is brought into it, the music nearly stops. There are no new songs, only reprises of earlier ones. Here *The Sound of Music* breaks from musical

comedies' tradition of accompanying the formation of a couple with a new song, and sometimes (in robust heterosexual spirit) even giving 'birth' to a new dance, such as the Continental in *The Gay Divorcee* (1934) or the Piccolino in *Top Hat*. With *The Sound of Music*, that sense of joyful, sensual potential is stifled all the more for giving the wedding its large-scale, public and institutionalised setting: the only other similar scene occurs as the family is forced to perform at the music festival, hinting at a parity between the two events.

Because Maria and Georg's coupling does not result in any new 'productions', they are somewhat de(hetero)sexualised in the process. Maria, in particular, is shorn of her quirky gender traits, youthful spirit and independence. Once she becomes Baroness von Trapp, her movements are stiff, controlled – twirling would be unthinkable now. Moreover, Andrews/Maria is now restricted to passive, supportive singing roles that serve the needs of the family, mothering Liesl in the reprise of 'Sixteen Going on Seventeen', and supporting her children and husband at the festival. Such is Camelot after the fall.

Sedate and sedated

4 Afterlife and Influence

So quickly was *The Sound of Music* taken up in popular culture that its afterlife began before it ever left the theatres. Soaring popularity and profits led to endless streams of reviews and articles entitled 'The Sound of Money', including the 1966 parody in *Mad* magazine. The movie's original run lasted so long that frustrated filmgoers in the UK and US started demanding that local theatre owners bring in new films and save everyone from the sweet scourge of *The Sound of Music*. (Such references to its sugar content were as relentless as puns on its title; Judith Crist warned 'calorie-counters, diabetics and grown-ups from eight to 80 had best beware'.[98])

Initially, *The Sound of Music* was treated as a stand-alone movie, a respected (or reviled) relic performed whole, on stages and TV. When the film was reproduced, it was reproduced intact, as

when Fox sent re-recorded prints around the globe all accompanied by the same publicity slogan, 'The Happiest Sound in the World', which was usually translated word for word. It was the same big film, after all. It didn't take long for Hollywood's *The Sound of Music* to become a master referent, eclipsing even its own prehistories in the Broadway show, the German films and the actual Trapp family history. In fact, the film consolidated its

German advert for *The Sound of Music*

own cultural authority with such force that people tend to view all its antecedents as variations of *it*.

Today, the 'film at large' remains the same, despite modest modifications, such as cuts to shorten its running time for TV broadcasts, or to make the nuns more acceptable to French censors, or to erase digitally Charmian Carr's bandaged ankle. But, if the original *The Sound of Music* enjoys the kind of historical and physical stability unknown to less prominent films (which often get recut, damaged or lost), it no longer claims the stern authority it once did, and over the decades, references to it have grown more informal and cheekier (the *Singalong* experience among them). Signs of the still-deep reverence for the movie now appear in more relaxed forms of cultural expression. New media technologies and viewing habits have helped change the playing field. In the 1980s, music videos enabled audiences – especially younger ones – to consume what were effectively musicals in miniature, as did musical episodes of non-musical television shows such as *Xena: Warrior Princess* (1995–2001), *Ally McBeal* (1997–2002) and *How I Met Your Mother* (2005–14), along with the musical parodies in *The Simpsons* (1989–) and other shows. The US sitcom *Will & Grace* (1998–2006) devoted an entire episode to *The Sound of Music* entitled 'Von Trapped'. (Apparently, the film will always be susceptible to puns.) By the late twentieth and early twenty-first centuries, *The Sound of Music* benefited from the renewed popularity of musicals on London and New York stages, with audiences returning en masse to huge hits like *Phantom of the Opera*, *Les Misérables* and *Wicked*. Fifty years after its release in film theatres, the musical genre, and with it, *The Sound of Music*, got its groove back.

The Sound of Music has always meant different things to different people, and has provoked a range of responses, whether from repeat viewers or diabetes-fearing detractors. There are Julie Andrews fetishists who have devoted a blog to an alternative universe of her film castings; in the realm of high art, choreographer Doug Elkins developed his critically acclaimed dance 'Fräulein Maria' in an affectionate homage to the film. *The Sound of Music*'s treatment in

the hands of LGBT cultures is especially fun. One commentator reminisced about a theme party 'in a gay crack house' with tag lines such as: 'I am Sixteen Going Down on Seventeen' and 'These Are a Few of My Favourite Queens'. In 2007, a scholarly piece entitled 'Julie Andrews Made Me Gay' was published.[99]

The Sound of Music is just as at home in staid, conservative contexts, with legions of fans among school and church groups and families (especially in innumerable mother and daughter bonding experiences); it has taken part in the tourism industry, with the bulging 'Sound of Music' tour in tiny Salzburg or the Trapp Family Lodge in Stowe, Vermont. And of course, it has always been appreciated by those in the Hollywood industry and by musical lovers and scholars, all of whom carry different personal attachments (or repulsions). For the communities to whom the original movie never spoke, it has

Debra Messing in *Will & Grace* ('Von Trapped' episode, 2006)

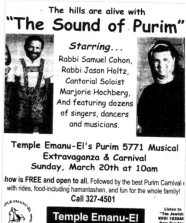

The hills are alive with

"The Sound of Purim"

Starring...
Rabbi Samuel Cohon,
Rabbi Jason Holtz,
Cantorial Soloist
Marjorie Hochberg,
And featuring dozens
of singers, dancers
and musicians.

**Temple Emanu-El's Purim 5771 Musical
Extravaganza & Carnival
Sunday, March 20th at 10am**

Show is FREE and open to all. Followed by the best Purim Carnival
with rides, food-including hamantashen, and fun for the whole family!
Call 327-4501

Temple Emanu-El
225 N. Country Club Rd., Tucson
www.templeemanueltucson.org

Listen to
"Too Jewish"
KVOI 1030AM
9am Sunday

been made to do so. Online digital cultures have offered trenchant, hilarious parodies, such as a fake trailer called 'The Sound of Music in the Ghetto' and a publicity image for 'The Sound of Death Metal' featuring Maria on her hill joyfully toting oversized guns. Regional and local permutations show great wit in their references. In the early 2000s, a Tucson (Arizona) synagogue put on 'The Sound of Purim', promoting it with a photo of a Jewish man in a habit and wimple.

Like much of US pop culture – and especially a movie effectively synonymous with Americana – traces of *The Sound of Music* are scattered all around the globe and across cinemas worldwide. Takashi Miike's 2001 *The Happiness of the Katakuris* is a frantic clay-animation and live 'splatter musical' that tells the story of a hotelier's family in a bucolic 'Alpine' setting in Japan.[100] Despite serialised murders, guest deaths and zombies, the singing family is steadfastly cheerful, even after a nearby 'Alp' unleashes a flood of molten lava upon them. Slightly more indirect is the film's connection to the 1970s *Lederhosenfilm* soft-core genre in Germany, with Tyrolean settings, costumes and eroticised yodelling. (As of this

Maria Goes Gunning; 'The Sound of Purim'

writing, surprisingly there are no direct pornographic parodies of *The Sound of Music*. Viewers will have to be content with the 2010 film *Mary Pops In: The Magical Nanny*.)

More serious was *The Sound of Mumbai: A Musical* (2010), which was not, in fact, a musical but a documentary about ghetto children who had the opportunity to perform songs from *The Sound of Music* accompanied by a live symphonic orchestra in downtown Mumbai. Using the original film's own underscoring (but not its songs – rights might well have been too expensive), *The Sound of Mumbai* demonstrates how *The Sound of Music* moves multi-directionally: the film's influence reached India, where it was repurposed and sent out internationally once more, rewiring its feelings of hope and uplift for a global context. But in similarity is difference, and, as an opening voiceover compellingly states, 'It would be easy to say, "If they [the children] believe in their dreams, they will do it." That would be the American way. But this isn't America, this is India.'

The Sound of Music provided a thematic thread throughout Lars von Trier's *Dancer in the Dark* (2000) where it offered a sense of escape for Selma, a lower-class immigrant living in an American small town in the mid-1960s. The hope that Selma invests in musicals in general, and *The Sound of Music* in particular, proves fraudulent, even cruel, and the movie ends with her swinging at the end of a hangman's noose.[101] Another art film popular at the time, Baz Luhrmann's *Moulin Rouge* (2000) used *The Sound of Music* as one of its numerous cultural references. Beaming sincerity, Ewan McGregor's character stumbles on the lyrics to 'The Sound of Music' when his friends begin work on an 'Alpine musical', a poetic inspiration that is, of course, familiar enough to bring audiences into the joke. In 2004, two years before *Will & Grace*, a comic movie entitled *Von Trapped* aired on British television that followed a hairdresser who'd been jilted watching *The Sound of Music*. So fraught was her ensuing obsession with the film, she travels to Salzburg in hopes of a cure.

These references dramatise three facts about *The Sound of Music* today: first, its long-standing, large-scale circulation has made it into an

abundantly easy point of cultural reference and quotation; second, audiences' attachments to the film and its songs seem to be unlimited; and third, its song repertoire – even the smallest fraction of a single piece – is enough to conjure up the entire *Sound of Music* phenomenon. And so the film continually gets readjusted, resized and reconfigured, encouraging new meanings and feelings for viewers, particularly when they are themselves the 'media-makers', putting elements of the film into unexpected contexts, such as 'Sound of Music in the Ghetto', or the 'Do Re Mi' flash mob in Antwerp's train station that went viral in 2009, and the hundreds of other partial *Sound of Music* re-enactments.

For musical historian Tamsen Wolff, an important measure of a musical's success is the extent to which its songs are repeated and imitated.[102] By that standard, *The Sound of Music* is probably the most successful musical ever made. In the 1960s and 70s, dozens of pop stars, crooners and jazz musicians, probable and improbable alike, recorded individual numbers from the show. The greatest concentration of songs tended to appear on Christmas LPs (or TV specials), performed by singers ranging from Andy Williams to Alvin and the Chipmunks. Throughout most of the 1970s and 80s, however, the tunes largely fell under the radar, before resurfacing in the 90s, an absence that corresponds to the unpopularity of film musicals at the time. That said, I would argue that *The Sound of Music* was less 'off

Baz Luhrmann's Alpine musical in *Moulin Rouge* (2004)

the grid' during this period than simply being enjoyed in private, unofficial forums and social rituals. After all, it has been an iconic text for generations of children, or of adults reliving their own youths, or in celebrating gay and religious affinities. And it has enjoyed an especially vibrant following among those who simply relish musicals, or Julie Andrews or, perhaps, even the Baroness.

It would take another book to detail the afterlives of *The Sound of Music*. One song alone, 'Do Re Mi', has had cameos in pop songs such as Madonna's 'Deeper and Deeper' or dialogue on shows like *The Simpsons*, when Bart says 'D'oh! A deer', or Belgian flash mobs. Still, it's worth checking to see how each of the songs has helped give the musical its prolonged emotional afterlife.

'Maria' is one of the context- and character-specific numbers in the show and has therefore not exerted much post-film musical influence. But it has had a robust iconic one, thanks in no small part to the idea of putting nuns into musical comedies (its impact on subsequent musicals such as *Sister Act* [1992] goes without saying).

There haven't been many musical covers of 'I Have Confidence' since 1965, but Andrews's performance is evoked from time to time. In *Will & Grace*'s 'Von Trapped', Grace/Debra Messing attends a screening wearing a kooky dress and hat that captures Maria's hideous outfit perfectly. In 2010, a small Belgian film, *Romantics Anonymous*/*Les Émotifs anonymes*, follows the blossoming romance

'I Have Confidence' homage in *Les Émotifs anonymes* (2010)

between two sensitive co-workers in a chocolate factory, one of whom resurrects 'Confidence' with surprising fidelity. Trey Parker and Matt Stone's Broadway musical *The Book of Mormon* paid homage to 'Confidence' in the number 'I Believe'. Facing a new life in Africa, the show's American evangelists transform lyrics such as 'A captain with seven children/what's so fearsome about that?' into 'A warlord who shoots people in the face/what's so scary about that?'

'Sixteen Going on Seventeen' has been revisited more frequently as a punchline than as a tune – and largely through Hammerstein's lyrics over Rodgers's music, as in the case of the verbal adjustments made at the gay *Sound of Music* theme party. Still, it has had few official covers.

The most frequently reprised number is 'My Favorite Things', even if it still appears in far too many holiday performances, such as those by Barry Manilow or when it aired in a special Christmas episode of *Glee* (2009–). Audiences have heard it clucked out by Björk in *Dancer in the Dark* and ferociously drummed by Outkast in a jazz/hip-hop fusion version. The piece has even appeared on TV in adverts for Dove hair conditioner and Victoria's Secret.

Although 'My Favorite Things' has given rise to some exceptional versions (John Coltrane's rendition comes immediately to mind), it has also provided a rich source for parody. Two involve Julie Andrews, who, while entwined with *The Sound of Music* as its official guide and muse, is rarely its satirist. Forty years after the film, lyrics to a 'blue-haired version' of 'Favorite Things' appeared online, including verses like:

When the pipes leak, when the bones creak,
When the knees go bad,
I simply remember my favourite things,
And then I don't feel so bad …

'Imagine that you are a blue-haired Julie Andrews singing it,' wrote one commentator, and reports soon followed that Dame Julie had actually performed it in 2004 on her birthday at an American Association of Retired Persons benefit at Radio City Music Hall. The story is not true: Andrews's ability to sing had been ruined by botched vocal cord surgery the previous decade, but fans, especially ageing baby boomers, found it easy to believe. 'What a great sense of humour!' said one. 'That's our Julie! Still great after all these years!'

More humorous is a parody Andrews was involved in herself before making the film. In June 1962, she joined friend Carol Burnett for a Carnegie Hall show that included a skit on a singing Swiss family, 'The Pratt Family', that opened with a few robust yodels and an endless stream of lederhosen-clad young men prancing around as Andrews and Burnett sang numbers such as 'The Things We Like Best', the lyrics of which kept cycling back to two 'favourite things': 'pigs' feet and cheese'.

Gwen Stefani's video for 'Wind It Up' was an extensive mash-up that riffed on the refrain from 'The Lonely Goatherd' and used visual imagery including nuns' habits, large iron gates and fake green hills. Campy though it was, it was less a parody than quirky homage (Stefani openly stated her respect for both the song and Andrews). In the late 1970s, Andrews had reprised 'Goatherd' in an appearance on *The Muppets* (1976–81) TV show. *The Sound of Music*'s other novelty song, 'So Long, Farewell', on the other hand, is unique for having no traceable public recordings beyond the film.

'Something Good' – again, not Rodgers's strongest number – was transformed by the popular Brazilian singer Caetano Veloso when he recorded a stripped-down version for his CD *A Foreign Sound* in 2004. Performing in English, Veloso's light, softly accented vocals, accompanied by a solo acoustic guitar, give the song a poignancy it lacks in the film.

In the early 1960s, 'Climb Ev'ry Mountain' thrived in the capable hands of vocalists such as Tony Bennett and Shirley

Gwen Stefani's 'Wind It Up' (2006)

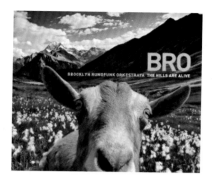

Bassey, and since then has continued to appear in the repertoire of singers.

Still, 'Mountain' has not enjoyed the autonomy apart from the show that the similar 'quest song' 'Impossible Dream' has from *Man of La Mancha*.

In 2011, the Brooklyn Rundfunk Orkestrata released a well-received CD *The Hills Are Alive*, turning the numbers from *The Sound of Music* into a fascinating, jazzy stew of pop, hip hop and blues. Showing how much *The Sound of Music* phenomenon has evolved with the times, even in the minds of its own producers and financial gatekeepers, the recording received the full blessing of the Rodgers and Hammerstein Organisation.

An especially delightful adaption of 'The Sound of Music' appears in the 2012 Australian film *Mental* by PJ Hogan. Opening with a swooping aerial shot of Australian mountaintops, the camera lands on red-headed, middle-aged Shirley (Rebecca Gibney) singing 'The Sound of Music' as she twirls in her yard full of hung laundry. After a slightly unhinged nanny figure arrives to help with her cluster of embarrassed children, Shirley finally sends her absentee husband Barry (Anthony LaPaglia) packing. Later, however, she agrees to make a wifely public appearance to help his local political campaign, under one condition: that he sing 'Edelweiss'. And so he does. LaPaglia speak-sings the number in front of his dumbfounded political supporters with even more tentativeness than Plummer.

However we may approach *The Sound of Music*, it is the songs that always have the last say. As the basis of our 'emotional memories' of the film, and of so many other references to it, the songs ground *The Sound of Music* phenomenon. They did this during the

Brooklyn Rundfunk Orkestrata's tribute CD

Opening of PJ Hogan's *Mental* (2012)

film's initial release and now, a half-century later, as it erupts in completely new social and media contexts. Whether performed and consumed in theatres, on stages, in people's homes or at parties, in schools, churches or clubs, or whether as officially released covers or unofficial online variations, it's these numbers that solidify *The Sound of Music* as a 'film classic'.

Notes

Abbreviations used: **EL** – Ernest Lehman Collection, Cinematic Arts Library, University of Southern California; **RR** – Richard Rodgers Collection, Performing Arts Collection, New York Public Library; **RW** – Robert Wise Collection, Cinematic Arts Library, University of Southern California.

1 Charmian Carr, with Jean A. S. Strauss, *Forever Liesl: A Memoir of* The Sound of Music (Thorndike, ME: Thorndike Press, 2000), p. 335.
2 <http://www.boxofficemojo.com/movies/?id=soundofmusic.htm>. Accessed 1 February 2015.
3 Richard Rodgers, letter to Harold Prince and Stephen Sondheim, 3 June 1970. Correspondence N–Z, Box 4, Folder 26 'Correspondence – Miscellaneous S (1947–75)' (RR).
4 Richard Rodgers, 'Preface', in Oscar Hammerstein II, *Lyrics by Oscar Hammerstein II* (Milwaukee, WI: Hal Leonard Books, 1985), p. xvii.
5 Quoted in Timothy D. Taylor, *The Sounds of Capitalism: Advertising, Music, and the Conquest of Culture* (Chicago: University of Chicago Press, 2012), p. 111.
6 Pauline Kael, *Kiss Kiss Bang Bang* (Toronto: Bantam, 1969), p. 215.
7 Quoted in Sergio Leeman, *Robert Wise on His Films* (Los Angeles: Silman-James Press, 1995), p. 8.
8 Oscar Andrew Hammerstein, *The Hammersteins: A Musical Theatre Family* (New York: Black Dog and Leventhal, 2010), p. 103.
9 Ibid., p. 114.
10 Richard Rodgers, letter to Robert Schuler Productions, 16 December 1970.

Correspondence N–Z, Box 4, Folder 25 'Correspondence – Miscellaneous S (1947–75)' (RR).
11 Hammerstein, *Lyrics*, p. 17.
12 Quoted in Hammerstein, *The Hammersteins*, p. 195.
13 Raymond Knapp compares the two films in his outstanding *The American Film Musical and the Formation of National Identity* (Princeton, NJ: Princeton University Press, 2005), pp. 230–50.
14 Michel Chion, *La Musique au cinéma* (Paris: Fayard, 1995), p. 317.
15 Bosley Crowther, 'The Soundness of Musicals: Musical Films', *New York Times*, 7 March 1965, section x, p. 1.
16 Robert Wise, 'Preface', in Julia Antopol Hirsch, *The Sound of Music: The Making of America's Favorite Movie* (New York: McGraw Hill, 1993), p. x.
17 Jeffrey Shandler, *While America Watches: Televising the Holocaust* (Oxford: Oxford University Press, 1999), p. 83.
18 Maria von Trapp, *The Story of the Trapp Family Singers* (New York: Harper, 2002), pp. 9, 11.
19 Mary Martin, *My Heart Belongs* (New York: William Morrow, 1976), p. 239.
20 George F. Custen, *Twentieth Century's Fox: Darryl F. Zanuck and the Culture of Hollywood* (New York: Basic Books, 1997), p. 359.
21 Quoted in Hirsch, *Sound of Music*, p. 8.
22 Russel Crouse and Howard Lindsay, 'Sound of Music Contract', 31 May 1961. Box 28 'Sound of Music Outlines', Folder 'Contract Memos' (RW).
23 Quoted in Leeman, *Robert Wise*, p. 7.
24 Ibid., p. 4.
25 Quoted in Hirsch, *Sound of Music*, p. 13.

26 Rudy Belmer, *Shoot the Rehearsal! Behind the Scenes with Assistant Director Reggie Callow* (Lanham, MD: Scarecrow Press, 2010), p. 130.

27 Saul Chaplin, *The Golden Age of Movie Musicals and Me* (Norman: University of Oklahoma Press, 1994), p. 177.

28 Christopher Plummer, *In Spite of Myself: A Memoir* (New York: Vintage, 2012), p. 393.

29 Chaplin, *Golden Age*, p. 213.

30 Robert Wise, miscellaneous notes, no date. Box 23 'The Sound of Music', Folder 12 'SOM Casting Notes' (RW).

31 Chaplin, *Golden Age*, p. 211.

32 Robert Wise, letter to Stuart Lyons at Fox in London, 9 December 1963. Box 'The Sound of Music', Folder 23.7 'Mike Kaplan' (RW).

33 Chaplin, *Golden Age*, p. 221.

34 Howard Lindsay and Russel Crouse, letter to Robert Wise, 5 February 1963. Box 'The Sound of Music', Folder 23.1 'Script Materials' (RW).

35 Robert Wise, letter to Lee Wallace, 24 February 1964. Box 'The Sound of Music', Folder 23.7 'Mike Kaplan' (RW).

36 Lindsay and Crouse, Folder 'Contract Memos' (RW).

37 Chaplin, *Golden Age*, p. 214.

38 Robert Wise, letter to Richard Zanuck, 30 September 1964. Box 'The Sound of Music', Folder 23.7 'Mike Kaplan' (RW).

39 Ernest Lehman, script outlines (folder dated 20 May 1963, yet ms. pages noted as 15 May 1963). Box 28 'SOM Outlines' (no folder numbers), pp. 12, 4 (EL).

40 Lindsay and Crouse, letter to Robert Wise.

41 Lehman, script outlines, p. 11.

42 Wise, miscellaneous notes, 'SOM Casting Notes' (RW).

43 Chaplin, *Golden Age*, p. 219.

44 Robynn Stilwell, 'The Television Musical', in Raymond Knapp, Mitchell Morris and Stacy Wolf (eds), *The Oxford Handbook of the American Musical* (Oxford: Oxford University Press, 2011), p. 159.

45 Wise, letter to Stuart Lyons.

46 Joshua Morrison assisted in writing portions of this chapter.

47 Ernest Lehman, first draft, 10 December 1963. Box 1 'The Sound of Music', Folder 'Sound of Music 3', p. 1 (EL).

48 Ibid.

49 Saul Chaplin, notes on recording foreign vocals, 11 March 1965. Box 28 'Sound of Music Outlines', Folder 'Notes on Foreign Dubbing' (EL).

50 Hammerstein, *Lyrics*, p. 26.

51 Richard Rodgers, liner notes to CD recording of Original Cast Recording of *The Sound of Music* (1959), p. 11.

52 Ibid.

53 Philip K. Scheuer, 'A Capsule Movie Tour of Europe and Zanuck', *Los Angeles Times*, 28 June 1964, p. T1; and Hedda Hopper, 'Edwards Will Film Story of Champion', *Los Angeles Times*, 5 November 1964, p. C11.

54 Frank Ferguson, letter to Richard Zanuck, 29 February 1963. Box 'SOUND OF MUSIC', Folder 'Saul Chaplin Personal Folder 23.3' (RW).

55 Quoted in Leeman, *Robert Wise*, p. 181.

56 Ernest Lehman, revisions to first draft, 25 October 1963. Box 'The Sound of Music', Folder 2 'Playscripts', p. 14A (RW).

57 Chaplin, *Golden Age*, p. 215.
58 Ibid., p. 216.
59 Ibid.
60 Ibid., p. 217.
61 Ibid.
62 Wise gave Maria the cameo in part to please her and in part to get her off his back. After the experience, the Baroness announced that she did not care at all for film-making.
63 Lehman, script outlines, p. 2.
64 Ernest Lehman, first draft screenplay, 6 March 1963. Box 'Sound of Music', Folder 3.13.3, pp. 15–16 (EL).
65 Agathe von Trapp, *Memories Before and After* The Sound of Music (New York: Harper, 2004), pp. 84–5.
66 Adrienne L. McLean, private conversation with the author, April 2012.
67 I am again indebted to Joshua Morrison for his observations about cues in orchestration regarding Liesl's move into maturity.
68 Ernest Lehman, first draft, 25 October 1963. Box 'SOUND OF MUSIC', Folder 2 'Playscripts – 1 First Draft', p. 31 (RW).
69 Quoted in Fred Bronson, The Sound of Music *Family Scrapbook* (London: Carlton, 2011), p. 19.
70 Ibid., p. 21.
71 Chaplin, notes on recording foreign vocals.
72 Quoted in Lewis Porter, *John Coltrane: His Life and Music* (Ann Arbor: University of Michigan Press, 1998), p. 184.
73 Carr, *Forever Liesl*, p. 50.
74 Ibid., p. 51.
75 Lehman, script outlines, section 3, part 1, p. 4.
76 Chaplin, *Golden Age*, p. 213.

77 Mike Kaplan, letter to Robert Wise, 13 March 1964. Box 'The Sound of Music', Folder 'Mike Kaplan 23.7' (RW).
78 Robert Wise, 'Editing', letter to Richard Zanuck, 30 September 1964. Box 'The Sound of Music', Folder 'Mike Kaplan 23.7' (RW).
79 Carr, *Forever Liesl*, p. 142.
80 Lehman, first draft screenplay, p. 7.
81 Lehman, script outlines, p. 10.
82 D. A. Miller, *Place for Us* (Cambridge, MA: Harvard University Press, 1998).
83 Quoted in Carr, *Forever Liesl*, p. 90.
84 My thanks to Phil Hallman for drawing this to my attention.
85 Hammerstein, *Lyrics*, p. 20.
86 Ibid., p. 13.
87 Ibid., pp. 29–30.
88 Quoted in Hirsch, *The Sound of Music*, p. 147.
89 Wise, 'Editing'.
90 Quoted in Leeman, *Robert Wise*, p. 182.
91 Saul Chaplin, letter to Frank Ferguson, 30 January 1964. Box 1 'The Sound of Music', Folder 'Saul Chaplin "Memos"' (EL).
92 Richard Dyer, 'The Sound of Music', *Movie* no. 23 (1976), p. 37.
93 Howard Lindsay and Russel Crouse, letter to Baroness Maria Augusta von Trapp, 15 July 1959. Vincent J. Donehue Papers, T-Mss 967, Box 002, Folder 'Notes on Rough Draft of SOUND OF MUSIC play' (RW).
94 Andrews quoted in Hirsch, *Sound of Music*, p. 157.
95 Lehman, script outlines, p. 15.
96 Chaplin, notes on recording foreign vocals.
97 Marni Nixon, with Stephen Cole, *I Could Have Sung All Night: My Story*

(New York: Billboard Books, 2006), p. 163.

98 Judith Crist, 'If You Have Diabetes, Stay Away from This Movie', *New York Herald-Tribune*, 3 March 1965.

99 Brett Farmer, 'Julie Andrews Made Me Gay', *Camera Obscura* 65, vol. 22 no. 22 (2007), pp. 144–53.

100 Mike D'Angelo, <http://www.vitagraphfilms.com/Films/Happiness/IntroHappiness.htm>. Accessed 30 May 2014.

101 For a fuller discussion, see my 'Affect and Film Music in Wildly Uncaring Circumstances', in Diedrich Diederichsen and Constanze Ruhm (eds), *Immediacy and Non-Simultaneity: Utopia and Sound* (Vienna: Academy of Fine Arts, 2010), pp. 89–114.

102 Tamsen Wolff, 'Theater', in Knapp, Morris and Wolf, *Oxford Handbook of the American Musical*, p. 132.

Credits

The Sound of Music
USA/1965

Directed by
Robert Wise
Screenplay by
Ernest Lehman
**With the Partial Use
of Ideas by**
Georg Hurdalek
Director of Photography
Ted McCord
Film Editor
William Reynolds
Production Designed by
Boris Leven
Music by
Richard Rodgers
Lyrics by
Oscar Hammerstein II
**Additional Words and
Music by**
Richard Rodgers

© Argyle Enterprises,
Inc., Twentieth Century-
Fox Film Corporation
Production Companies
Twentieth Century-Fox
presents a Robert Wise
production of Rodgers
and Hammerstein's 'The
Sound of Music'

Associate Producer
Saul Chaplin
**Unit Production
Manager**
Saul Wurtzel
Assistant Director
Ridgeway Callow

**2nd Unit Supervision
[Austria]**
Maurice Zuberano
Additional Photography
Paul Beeson
**Special Photographic
Effects**
L. B. Abbott
Emil Kosa Jr
Puppeteers
Bil Baird
Cora Baird
Set Decorations
Walter M. Scott
Ruby Levitt
Vocal Supervision
Robert Tucker
Music Editor
Robert Mayer
Costumes Designed by
Dorothy Jeakins
Makeup by
Ben Nye
Hairstyles by
Margaret Donovan
**Music Supervised,
Arranged and
Conducted by**
Irwin Kostal
Choreography by
Marc Breaux
Dee Dee Wood
Sound by
Murray Spivack
[Music Mixer]
Bernard Freericks
[Sound Mixer]

**Sound Recording
Supervised by**
Fred Hynes
James Corcoran
Dialogue Coach
Pamela Danova
**Aerial Views
Photographed with an**
MCS-70 Camera

*From the Stage Musical
with*
Music and Lyrics by
Richard Rodgers
Oscar Hammerstein II
Book by
Howard Lindsay
Russel Crouse
**Originally Produced on
the Stage by**
Leland Hayward
Richard Halliday
Richard Rodgers
Oscar Hammerstein II

uncredited
Executive Producers
Richard D. Zanuck
Producer
Robert Wise
Unit Manager [Austria]
Laci von Ronay
2nd Assistant Director
Richard Lang
European Casting
Stuart Lyons
Camera Operator
Paul Lockwood
Script Supervisor
Betty Levin

Camera Technician
Roger Shearman Jr
Gaffer
Jack Brown
Best Boy Electric
Jack Dimmack
Key Grip
Walter Fitchman
Best Boy Grip
Fred Richter
Cable Operator
Jesse Long
Still Photography
James Mitchell
Assistant Art Director
Harry Kemm
Property Master
Eddie Jones
2nd Unit Properties
Don B. Greenwood
Sketch Artist
Maurice Zuberano
Costumer – Men
Dick James
Costumer – Women
Josephine Brown
Makeup
Willard Buell
Hairstyles
Ray Forman
Assistant Film Editor
Larry Allen
Sound Recordist
William Buffinger
Boom Operator
Orrick Barrett
Supervising Publicist
Mort Shuman
Unit Publicist (Argyle Enterprises)
Mike Kaplan

Head of European Publicity (Twentieth Century-Fox)
Fred Hift
Helicopter Pilot
Gilbert Chomat
Studio Chaperone
Jean Seaman

CAST
Julie Andrews
Maria Augusta Kutschera
Christopher Plummer
Captain Georg von Trapp
Richard Haydn
Max Detweiler
Peggy Wood
Mother Abbess
Anna Lee
Sister Margaretta, the Mistress of Postulants
Portia Nelson
Sister Berthe, the Mistress of Novices
Ben Wright
Herr Zeller
Daniel Truhitte
Rolf Gruber, delivery boy
Norma Varden
Frau Schmidt, von Trapp housekeeper
Marni Nixon
Sister Sophia
Gil Stuart
Franz, von Trapp butler
Evadne Baker
Sister Bernice
Doris Lloyd
Baroness Ebberfeld

Charmian Carr
Liesl von Trapp
Nicholas Hammond
Friedrich von Trapp
Heather Menzies
Louisa von Trapp
Duane Chase
Kurt von Trapp
Angela Cartwright
Brigitta von Trapp
Debbie Turner
Marta von Trapp
Kym Karath
Gretl von Trapp
the children

Eleanor Parker
Baroness Elsa Schrader

uncredited
Doreen Tryden
Sister Agatha
Dorothy Jeakins
nun
The Toby Reiser Quintet
Salzburg Festival contestants winning second prize
Alan Callow
young Nazi on festival stage
Bill Lee
singing voice of Captain von Trapp
Margery McKay
singing voice of Mother Abbess
Maria von Trapp
passerby

Filmed from 26 March to 20 August 1964 (with reshoots on 1 September 1964) for three weeks at 20th Century-Fox Studios (Los Angeles, California, USA), followed by ten weeks on location in Austria (Salzburg, Upper Austria and Salzkammergut) and Germany (Berchtesgaden in Bavaria), followed by a further six weeks filming at 20th Century-Fox Studios.
Budget c. $8,200,000.
65mm (Todd-AO); 2.35:1 (35mm prints); colour by DeLuxe; sound (Westrex Recording System – 35mm prints: mono/4-track stereo; 70mm prints: 6-track stereo). Released in both 70mm and 35mm formats. MPAA: 20734.

US theatrical release by Twentieth Century-Fox Film Corporation on 2 March 1965 (New York City premiere). Running time: 174 minutes. Re-released in 1973 and 1990.

UK theatrical release by 20th Century Fox Film Co. Ltd on 29 March 1965. BBFC certificate: U (no cuts). Running time: 170 minutes 0 seconds/19,125 feet.
UK theatrical re-release by 20th Century Fox Film Co. Ltd on 26 September 2007. BBFC certificate: U (no cuts). Running time: 174 minutes 20 seconds/15,689 feet + 6 frames.

Credits compiled by Julian Grainger